TECHNOLOGY

Studio Muti

Researched by
Simon Rogers

BPP

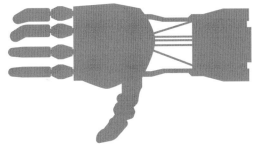

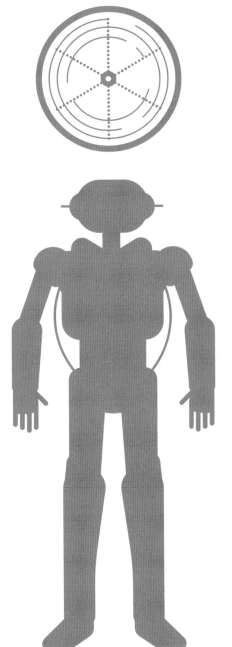
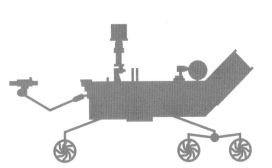

TECHNOLOGY

Studio Muti

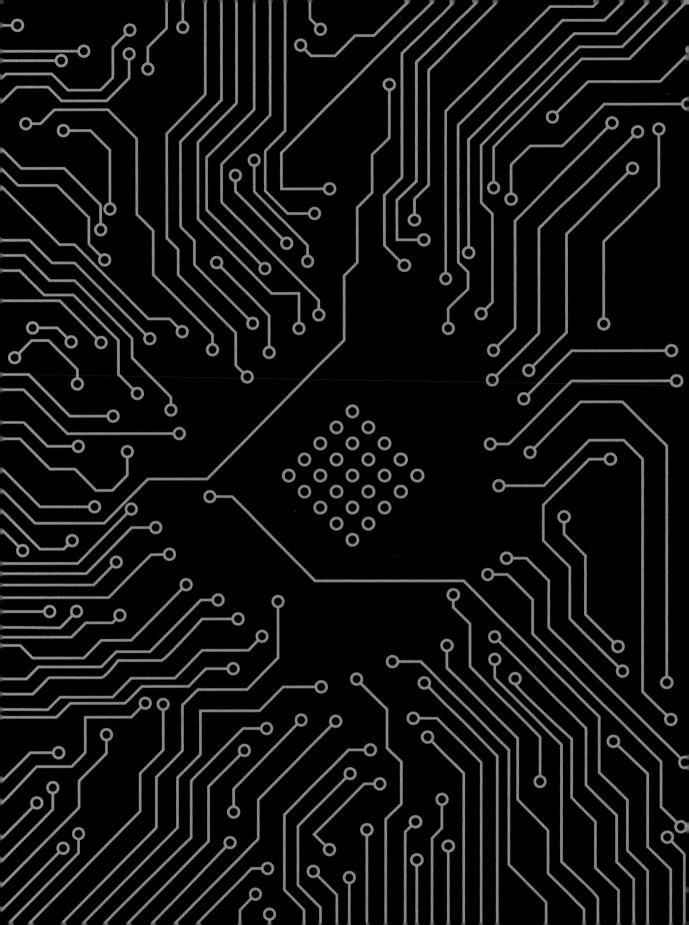

INTRODUCTION

Since the invention of the abacus in ancient
Sumeria nearly 5,000 years ago, technology has
developed beyond the realms of what could ever
have been imagined then.

From smartphones, drones and computers to long-
distance spacecraft, the tallest buildings in the
world and breakthroughs in new medicines, we are
surrounded by technology, and much of it is
relatively new. Up until the early 1900s people
travelled around the world in ships that took months
to reach their destination, not on airplanes, and the
first mobile phones only came into use in the 1970s.

There was a time when a computer could be the size
of a small house – today, a computer can fit on a
fingertip. In the 21st century it is almost impossible
to live without them – computers are in our homes
as laptops and tablets and built into our cars and
appliances.

In a hospital, machines can look inside our bodies
and robot surgeons may operate on us. On the road,
driverless cars detect their surroundings to navigate.
New developments are happening every day and
soon, technology may be unrecognisable again.

This book showcases the incredible technological
developments from the past, near-present and the
future possibilities in fascinating infographics. Turn
the page to get the low-down on technology...

HIGH-TECH WORLD

Every single man-made element of our world uses technology in some way.

Most technology feeds on power – and lots of it! As the number of electricity-hungry machines has rocketed, energy generation methods have had to keep up with demand. Though fossil fuels – coal, oil and gas – are still widely used, they are a limited resource that may run out in the near future. Renewable energy sources, such as wind, water and the Sun, are being harnessed more and more.

The infrastructure that supports urban areas and connects them via roads, bridges and tunnels requires technical designers and engineers to plan, model and test structures before a brick is even laid.

Keeping a close eye on the planet from high above in space are craft, monitoring every change in the ocean, the land and asteroids that may be drifting too close.

This chapter looks at the lifeblood of the modern world – energy – as well as the visible and invisible technology all around us.

ENERGY GENERATION

In the 1820s and 30s, English scientists made groundbreaking advances in the field of electro science. These included the development of the electric motor and electromagnets, which led to the use of electricity to power technology. Today, electricity is generated in huge amounts.

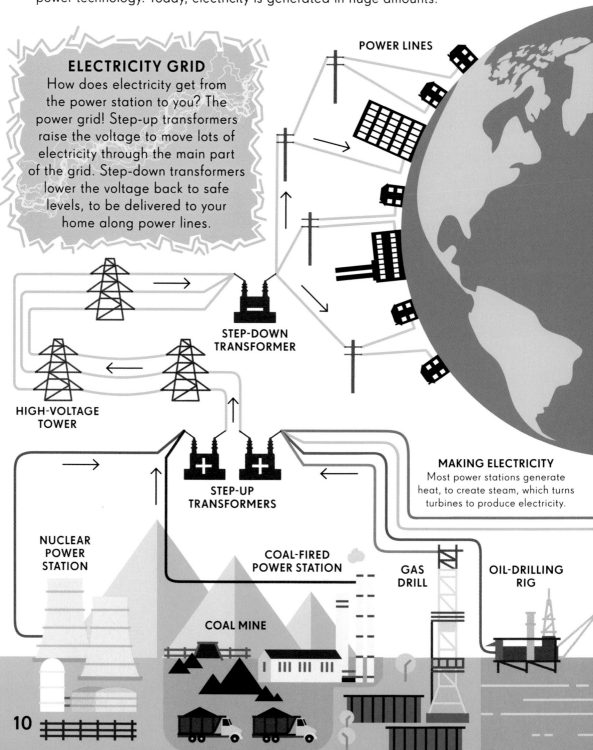

ELECTRICITY GRID

How does electricity get from the power station to you? The power grid! Step-up transformers raise the voltage to move lots of electricity through the main part of the grid. Step-down transformers lower the voltage back to safe levels, to be delivered to your home along power lines.

POWER LINES

STEP-DOWN TRANSFORMER

HIGH-VOLTAGE TOWER

STEP-UP TRANSFORMERS

MAKING ELECTRICITY
Most power stations generate heat, to create steam, which turns turbines to produce electricity.

NUCLEAR POWER STATION

COAL-FIRED POWER STATION

GAS DRILL

OIL-DRILLING RIG

COAL MINE

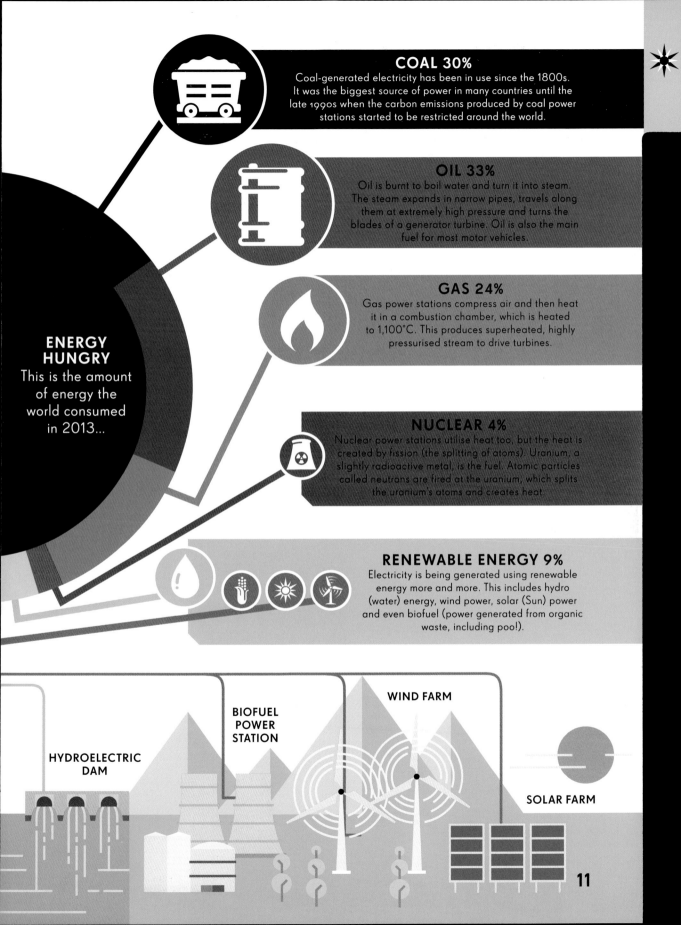

COAL 30%

Coal-generated electricity has been in use since the 1800s. It was the biggest source of power in many countries until the late 1990s when the carbon emissions produced by coal power stations started to be restricted around the world.

OIL 33%

Oil is burnt to boil water and turn it into steam. The steam expands in narrow pipes, travels along them at extremely high pressure and turns the blades of a generator turbine. Oil is also the main fuel for most motor vehicles.

GAS 24%

Gas power stations compress air and then heat it in a combustion chamber, which is heated to 1,100°C. This produces superheated, highly pressurised stream to drive turbines.

NUCLEAR 4%

Nuclear power stations utilise heat too, but the heat is created by fission (the splitting of atoms). Uranium, a slightly radioactive metal, is the fuel. Atomic particles called neutrons are fired at the uranium, which splits the uranium's atoms and creates heat.

RENEWABLE ENERGY 9%

Electricity is being generated using renewable energy more and more. This includes hydro (water) energy, wind power, solar (Sun) power and even biofuel (power generated from organic waste, including poo!).

ENERGY HUNGRY

This is the amount of energy the world consumed in 2013...

HYDROELECTRIC DAM

BIOFUEL POWER STATION

WIND FARM

SOLAR FARM

INFRASTRUCTURE

As well as electricity supply, roads, rail lines, tunnels and buildings make up the infrastructure all around us. The evermore complex and ingenious solutions to constructing it are indisputably triumphs of modern engineering and technology.

5 TALLEST BUILDINGS IN THE WORLD

BURJ KHALIFA
United Arab Emirates, 828m

SHANGHAI TOWER
China, 632m

CLOCK ROYAL TOWER
Saudi Arabia, 601m

ONE WORLD TRADE CENTER
USA, 541.3m

TAIPEI 101
China, 508m

Between the 87th and 92nd floors of **Taipei 101** hangs a huge 660-tonne steel pendulum. During typhoons or earthquakes, the pendulum sways to counteract the movement of the building.

LONGEST BRIDGE
Danyang-Kunshan Grand Bridge, China

HOW TO DIG A TUNNEL
Tunnel boring machines (TBMs) can cut through the ground at 120m a week.

Bored earth is sent back along the machine on a conveyor belt

Grippers grip the tunnel wall and hydraulic arms push the cutting head forwards

FRONT VIEW
The cutting head rotates to gouge through rock

New sections of tunnel wall are put in place

Rest rooms and offices

Conveyor belt

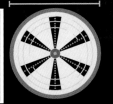

140m long (as long as two airplanes!)

BUILDING BRIDGES

Building bridges to span the widest rivers and valleys is a challenge. They must be designed to withstand the weight of thousands of vehicles, as well as extreme temperatures, strong winds and earthquakes. Here are six of the most incredible.

NOT TO SCALE

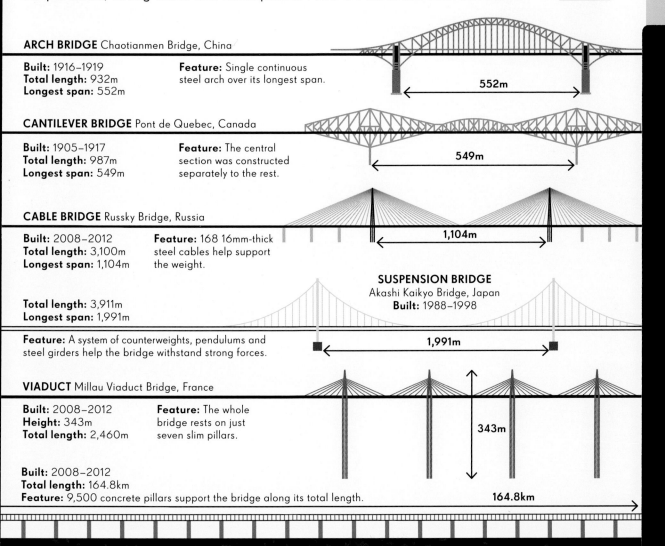

ARCH BRIDGE Chaotianmen Bridge, China

Built: 1916–1919
Total length: 932m
Longest span: 552m

Feature: Single continuous steel arch over its longest span.

552m

CANTILEVER BRIDGE Pont de Quebec, Canada

Built: 1905–1917
Total length: 987m
Longest span: 549m

Feature: The central section was constructed separately to the rest.

549m

CABLE BRIDGE Russky Bridge, Russia

Built: 2008–2012
Total length: 3,100m
Longest span: 1,104m

Feature: 168 16mm-thick steel cables help support the weight.

1,104m

SUSPENSION BRIDGE
Akashi Kaikyo Bridge, Japan
Built: 1988–1998

Total length: 3,911m
Longest span: 1,991m

Feature: A system of counterweights, pendulums and steel girders help the bridge withstand strong forces.

1,991m

VIADUCT Millau Viaduct Bridge, France

Built: 2008–2012
Height: 343m
Total length: 2,460m

Feature: The whole bridge rests on just seven slim pillars.

343m

Built: 2008–2012
Total length: 164.8km
Feature: 9,500 concrete pillars support the bridge along its total length.

164.8km

5 LONGEST TUNNELS IN THE WORLD

60.4km	Guangzhou Metro, Line 3, China
57.1km	Beijing Subway, Line 10, China
57.0km	Gotthard Base Tunnel, Swiss Alps
53.9km	Seikan Tunnel, Japan
50.5km	Channel Tunnel, UK and France

MONITORING EARTH

Technology helps us to monitor what is happening all around the world from space. Scientists use a network of sensitive equipment to measure the Earth's atmosphere, weather, oceans, sea ice and even passing asteroids.

EARTHQUAKES

The US Geological Survey monitors changes at the Earth's surface using creepmeters, strainmeters and tiltmeters. Instruments have been installed near active faults and volcanoes in California in the USA, Japan, China, Iceland and Italy.

SEA ICE

Sea ice is monitored by satellites using a microwave radiometer. This instrument measures the microwaves that radiate from the Earth and detects the difference between seawater and sea ice.

TERRAIN

Launched in 2007, German satellite TerraSAR-X's mission is to capture high-quality radar images of the entire Earth's surface. It circles the planet via the poles, taking close-up high-resolution pictures. These are stitched together to create large images.

CLOUDS

The CloudSat satellite is equipped with a radar 1,000 times more sensitive than existing weather satellites. CloudSat filmed the eye of Typhoon Fantala in the Indian Ocean in April 2016, giving scientists a glimpse directly into the storm.

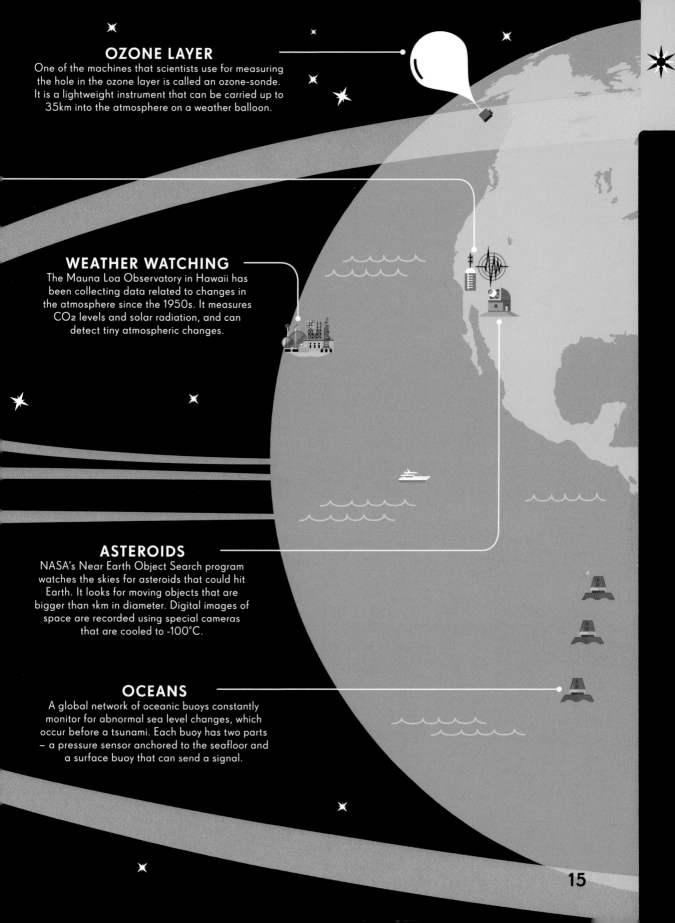

OZONE LAYER

One of the machines that scientists use for measuring the hole in the ozone layer is called an ozone-sonde. It is a lightweight instrument that can be carried up to 35km into the atmosphere on a weather balloon.

WEATHER WATCHING

The Mauna Loa Observatory in Hawaii has been collecting data related to changes in the atmosphere since the 1950s. It measures CO_2 levels and solar radiation, and can detect tiny atmospheric changes.

ASTEROIDS

NASA's Near Earth Object Search program watches the skies for asteroids that could hit Earth. It looks for moving objects that are bigger than 1km in diameter. Digital images of space are recorded using special cameras that are cooled to -100°C.

OCEANS

A global network of oceanic buoys constantly monitor for abnormal sea level changes, which occur before a tsunami. Each buoy has two parts – a pressure sensor anchored to the seafloor and a surface buoy that can send a signal.

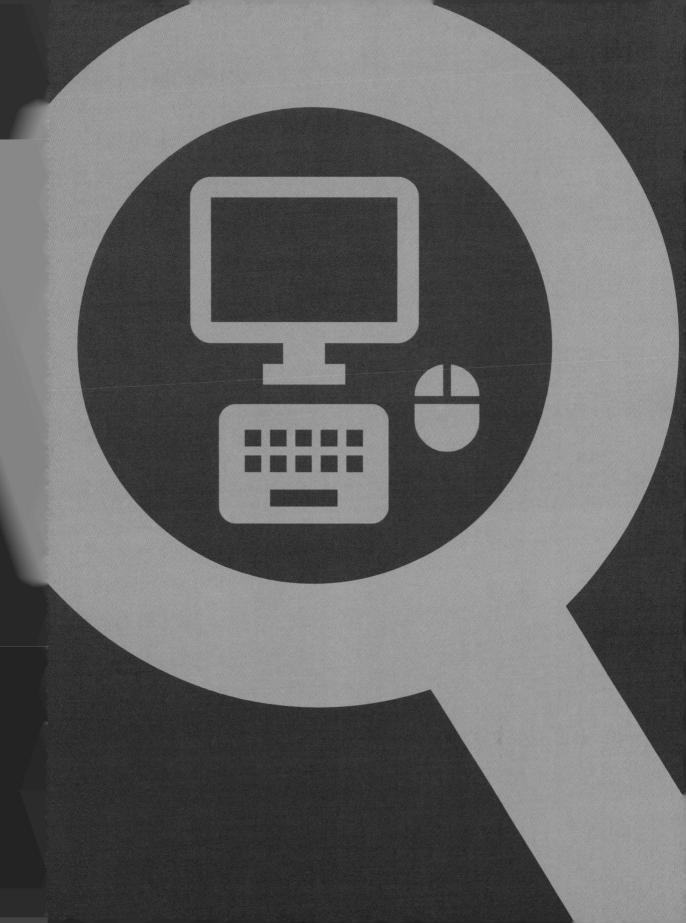

COMPUTERS

Not so long ago, a computer was a mammoth machine. Today, you have the same processing power in the palm of your hand.

It's a development that has happened fast – within a few decades we have gone from the basics of computing to devices that can perform thousands of functions and provide almost constant companionship. Yet few of us have any idea how these powerful machines work, and how they will continue to change.

Firstly, there are the mechanics – what does each part do? How do they stay cool?

Secondly, there's storage – as applications require more memory, finding ways to fit more on to our phones and laptops becomes ever more vital.

Then there's the Internet – increasingly the most significant way we interact and a part of our everyday routines.

Digital devices are at the centre of almost every interaction with the world today. Find out more about how we got here by turning the page.

FROM THE ABACUS...

Computers have come a long way from their surprisingly distant beginnings. Here are some of the groundbreaking inventions from 2000 BC to the present day.

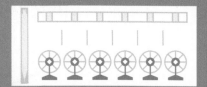

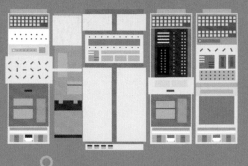

1642
French mathematician Blaise Pascal invented the **Pascaline** – a mechanical calculator that could add, subtract and multiply numbers using a set of dials.

1944
The gargantuan British computer **Colossus** was used to break Nazi codes during World War II. Huge decrypting computer the Turing Bombe and the room-sized Harvard Mark-1 were forerunners to this famous machine.

1950
The **IBM 650** was the first mass-produced computer. A machine could be built in a day and in all around 2,000 were produced.

MODERN COMPUTING

EARLY DEVICES
For thousands of years, humans have invented devices to automate sums. Around 1600 kinds of simple calculating machines were built.

1ST GENERATION
Machines could run thousands of calculations in one second, but they were big, bulky, slow and expensive.

2ND GENERATION
Smaller, but prone to overheating. The invention of the transistor in 1947 improved reliability.

c.AD 1200
The **equatorium** was an instrument used for calculating the positions of the Moon, Sun and planets.

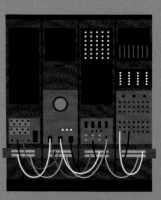

2400 BC
The **abacus** is the oldest-known calculating device. Made from a wooden frame, wire and beads, it can be used to make repeated calculations more quickly than the human brain.

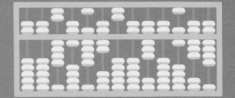

1946
ENIAC was the first all-electronic computer. It was also the fastest then in existence – this 27-tonne machine could process information 1,000 times faster than any other.

1956
The first fully transistorised computer was the **Harwell CADET**. The invention of the transistor was one of the most important developments in electronics and paved the way for the future.

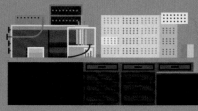

...TO THE TABLET

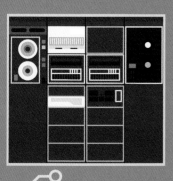

1970
One of the most successful computers ever made, the **PDP11** was sold up until the 1990s and it influenced the design of computers to come in the following decade.

1975
The **Altair 8800** was the first personal computer (PC). It came as a kit, meaning anyone could make one at home. It introduced the idea of a computer for the ordinary household.

1982
The **Commodore 64** is the best-selling computer model of all time, with more than 22 million sold.

1982
Grid Compass 1101 was the first laptop. It featured a 320 × 240-pixel display – tiny compared to today's computers.

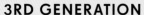

3RD GENERATION
Compact integrated circuits and silicon chips led to smaller, faster and more efficient computers.

FOURTH GENERATION
The generation of computers that we are familiar with today. They are smaller than ever before, increasingly fast, portable and connectable, and are equipped with tiny microprocessors.

1964
The **IBM 360** could perform data processing on a large scale, and advanced compatibility enabled many machines to function together in a 'computer network'.

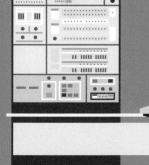

1977
The **Commodore PET** was the first mass-produced ready-made PC. It was stylish, user-friendly and it had a built-in display and cassette drive.

1980
The **Sinclair ZX80** pushed boundaries again. It had 1 kilobyte of memory and could be programmed by anyone using a simple computer language. It could also plug into a TV set.

2010
Apple launches the **iPad** – a compact, wireless portable 'tablet' computer with a touchscreen. Millions have been sold.

HOW DO COMPUTERS WORK?

We use computers every day, but how much do we know about how they work? What is a motherboard? How do computers stay cool? Here's your graphic guide to the basics of the hardware.

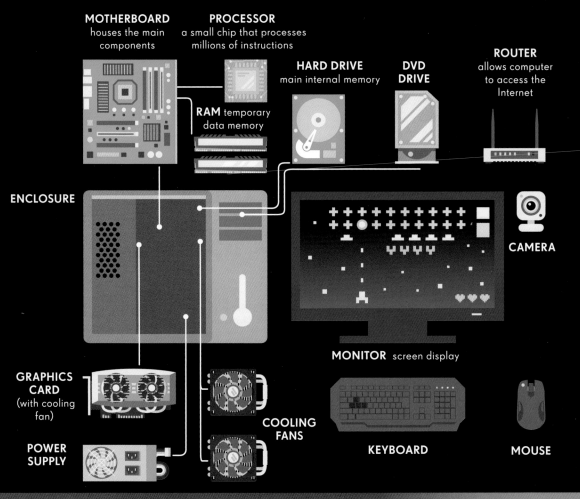

MOTHERBOARD houses the main components

PROCESSOR a small chip that processes millions of instructions

HARD DRIVE main internal memory

DVD DRIVE

ROUTER allows computer to access the Internet

RAM temporary data memory

ENCLOSURE

CAMERA

MONITOR screen display

GRAPHICS CARD (with cooling fan)

COOLING FANS

KEYBOARD

MOUSE

POWER SUPPLY

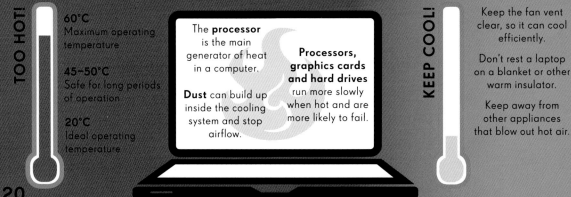

TOO HOT!

60°C Maximum operating temperature

45–50°C Safe for long periods of operation

20°C Ideal operating temperature

The **processor** is the main generator of heat in a computer.

Dust can build up inside the cooling system and stop airflow.

Processors, graphics cards and hard drives run more slowly when hot and are more likely to fail.

KEEP COOL!

Keep the fan vent clear, so it can cool efficiently.

Don't rest a laptop on a blanket or other warm insulator.

Keep away from other appliances that blow out hot air.

PORTABLE STORAGE

Computers need storage not only as a place to store files but as a space to process information. Hard drives and portable storage devices have shrunk smaller and smaller as their storage capacity has grown 50 million-fold. Here is storage past and present.

94mm
90mm

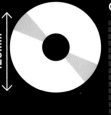

3.5-INCH FLOPPY DISK (1982)
Storage: 1.4MB

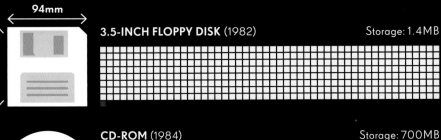

CD-ROM (1984)
Storage: 700MB

98mm
99mm

ZIP DRIVE (1994)
Storage: 100MB

120mm

DVD (1995)
Storage: 4.7GB

23mm
83mm

USB FLASH DRIVE (1999)
Storage: Up to 256GB

24mm
32mm

SD CARD (1999)
Storage: Up to 2GB

15mm
11mm

MICRO SDXC (2009)
Storage: Up to 2TB

THE CLOUD (2000s)
Storage: 1EB
A virtual storage system. Data is stored on remote servers, which can be accessed via the Internet without the need for separate portable storage hardware.

BIT
Single binary digit (1 or 0)

BYTE
8 bits = one character

KILOBYTE (KB)
1,000 bytes = short paragraph

MEGABYTE (MB)
1,000 kilobytes = short novel

GIGABYTE (GB)
1,000 megabytes = 7 minutes of HD video

TERABYTE (TB)
1,000 gigabytes = 50,000 trees made into paper and printed

PETABYTE (PB)
1,000 terabytes = 20 million 4-drawer filing cabinets filled with text

EXABYTE (EB)
1,000 petabytes = one-fifth of all of the words ever spoken by humans

THE INTERNET

The world has never been more connected, and it's down to the Internet — a worldwide system of computer networks transmitting information to billions of devices.

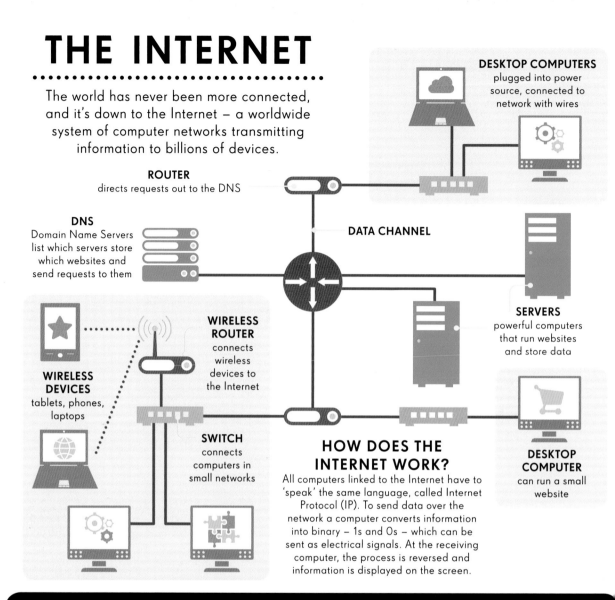

DESKTOP COMPUTERS
plugged into power source, connected to network with wires

ROUTER
directs requests out to the DNS

DNS
Domain Name Servers list which servers store which websites and send requests to them

DATA CHANNEL

SERVERS
powerful computers that run websites and store data

WIRELESS ROUTER
connects wireless devices to the Internet

WIRELESS DEVICES
tablets, phones, laptops

SWITCH
connects computers in small networks

DESKTOP COMPUTER
can run a small website

HOW DOES THE INTERNET WORK?

All computers linked to the Internet have to 'speak' the same language, called Internet Protocol (IP). To send data over the network a computer converts information into binary — 1s and 0s — which can be sent as electrical signals. At the receiving computer, the process is reversed and information is displayed on the screen.

GROWTH OF INTERNET USE

The Internet came into public use in 1993. Today, nearly half of the world's population use it.

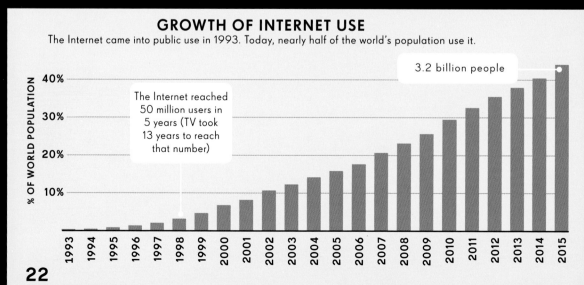

3.2 billion people

The Internet reached 50 million users in 5 years (TV took 13 years to reach that number)

% OF WORLD POPULATION

40%

30%

20%

10%

1993 1994 1995 1996 1997 1998 1999 2000 2001 2002 2003 2004 2005 2006 2007 2008 2009 2010 2011 2012 2013 2014 2015

EVERY MINUTE ON THE INTERNET...

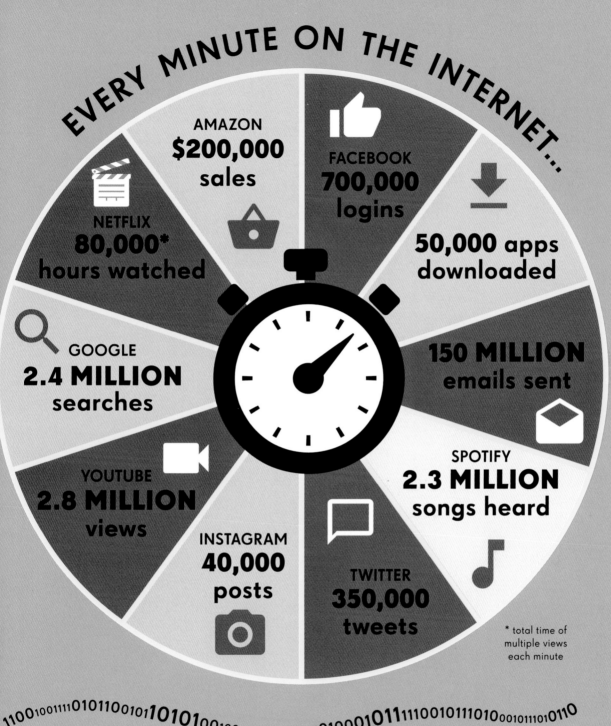

AMAZON
$200,000
sales

NETFLIX
80,000*
hours watched

FACEBOOK
700,000
logins

50,000 apps
downloaded

GOOGLE
2.4 MILLION
searches

150 MILLION
emails sent

YOUTUBE
2.8 MILLION
views

SPOTIFY
2.3 MILLION
songs heard

INSTAGRAM
40,000
posts

TWITTER
350,000
tweets

* total time of
multiple views
each minute

1100₁₀₀₁₁₁₁**0101**1001₀₁**1010100**₁₀₀₁₁₀₁₀₁₀₁₁₁₀₁₀₁**01000**₁**011**₁₁₁₀₀₁₀**111**₀₁₀₀₀₀₁₀₁₁₁₀₁**0110**

11010101**010001011**₁₁₁₀₀₁₀₁₁₁₀₁₀₀₀₁₁₁₁₀₁₁₀₁₀₁₀₀₁**1001010001**₀₁**01010111001001111001011**

SUPERCOMPUTERS

Some computing tasks require much more 'brain' power than the computers we use at home provide, and this is where supercomputers come in. These extraordinary machines possess almost unimaginable processing power.

SUPER CHAMPION

Name: IBM's Deep Blue

Built: 1989

Location: USA

Size: 2m tall

Cost: $100 million

Speed: 200 million chess positions per second

Memory: 32Gb

In 1996 Deep Blue became the first computer to beat a reigning world chess champion under competition conditions. IBM also built Watson, a computer that won $1 million on the US game show Jeopardy in 2011.

SUPER SMALL

Name: Michigan Micro Mote

Built: 2004

Location: USA

Size: 5mm x 2mm

Cost: Unknown

Speed: approximately 200 instructions per minute

Memory: 64 bits

A tiny solar-powered computer, half the size of a housefly. The Micro Mote's key function as a sensor or monitor has practical applications in medicine and personal security because it can go unnoticed

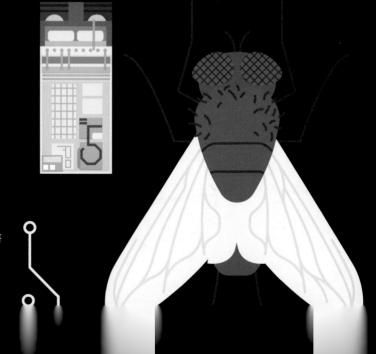

SUPER FAST

Name: Tianhe-2

Built: 2013

Location: China

Size: Several rooms

Cost: $390 million

Speed: 33,860 trillion calculations per second

Memory: 1.5PB

⭐ Held the record for the fastest computer in existence from June 2013 to June 2015. Tianhe-2 can be used to control traffic lights, predict earthquakes, design aircraft, create movie special effects and help with pollution control.

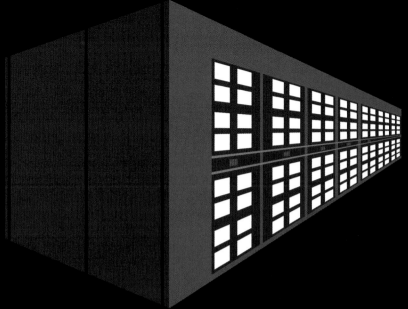

SUPER BIG

Name: SAGE (Semi-Automatic Ground Environment)

Built: 1957–1963

Location: 23 data centres across North America

Size: Each 4-storey, bombproof, windowless data centre had two CPUs (Central Processing Units), each taking up 700 sq m

Cost: $8–12 billion (in 1964)

Speed: 75,000 instructions per second

Memory: 256Kb per CPU

⭐ Defence system that monitored airborne threats to the USA during the Cold War (1947–1991). The data centre network was connected up to hundreds of radar stations, enabling fast deployment of defensive action.

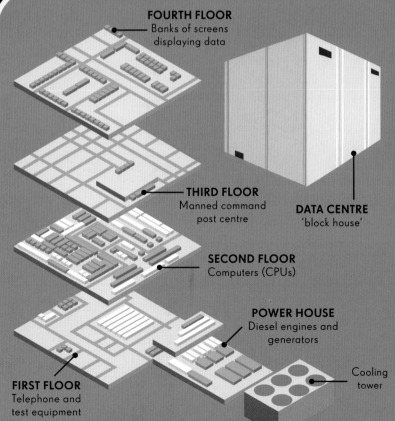

FOURTH FLOOR
Banks of screens displaying data

THIRD FLOOR
Manned command post centre

DATA CENTRE
'block house'

SECOND FLOOR
Computers (CPUs)

POWER HOUSE
Diesel engines and generators

Cooling tower

FIRST FLOOR
Telephone and test equipment

ROBOT AGE

Robots are the subject of many sci-fi movies, often shown as mechanical humanoids with two eyes, two legs and two arms. However, outside of fiction, robots come in all shapes and sizes and are used in almost every industry today.

In manufacturing items from food to cars, robotic machines are programmed to repeat actions thousands of times, exactly the same on each repetition, and without ever tiring. In dangerous war zones, remote-controlled machines can be sent in to defuse bombs. In hospitals, surgical robots can operate with the precision needed to carry out microsurgery. Robots are making our lives easier.

We can have robots in our homes – automatic vacuums can clean their way around rooms while we do other things. Robots can be used to explore the most extreme environments – the deepest depths of the oceans, the coldest places on Earth and even hundreds of millions of miles into space.

But a robot cannot yet interact like a human. It can't think like a human, have a conversation, or design and create something from scratch. Robots still need the human interaction of creation and direction to make them work. Take a look at the story of robotics...

ROBOTS IN HISTORY

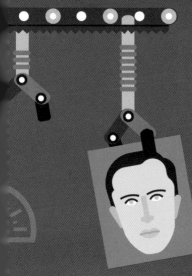

The roots of modern robotics can be traced back to the first automatons (mechanical humans) of the 9th century and mechanised contraptions from even earlier. The word 'robot' was coined in 1920 by Czech playwright Karel Capekis in his play *RUR* (*Rossum's Universal Robots*).

ROBOT: an automatic device that performs functions normally ascribed to humans or a machine in the form of a human. – K. Capekis

350 BC
Greek mathematician Archytas built a steam-propelled flying 'pigeon'.

AD 1495
A drawing in one of Da Vinci's sketchbooks appears to show a humanoid robot with movable parts*.

1700 ONWARDS
Countless automatons were created, many in the form of humans – one in the form of a duck!

*If it were to be remade, it is imagined to look like this.

1964
The Ranger 7 space probe was the first to send back close-up images of the Moon.

1994
Dante II, an eight-legged walking robot, was built to descend into dangerous volcanoes to collect samples.

1997
The Sojourner rover was the first roving robot to travel around and explore the surface of Mars.

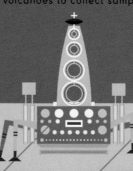

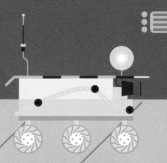

MOVIE BOTS

Robots have been on the big screen for nearly a century. Here are some of the most famous movie bots.

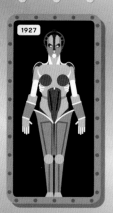

1927

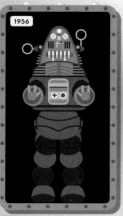

1956

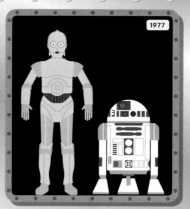

1977

2008

Maria (*Metropolis*)
One of the first female robot characters in sci-fi.

Robby (*Forbidden Planet*)
This iconic robot appeared in many more films and TV shows.

C3PO/R2D2 (*Star Wars*)
Humanoid C3PO and companion R2D2 help the heroes save the day.

Wall-E (Disney's *Wall-E*)
Wall-E's job is to clean up Earth after humans have wrecked it.

1913
The world's first automated conveyor belt assembly line was built by Henry Ford to manufacture cars.

1932
First robot toy, the 'Lilliput', was made in Japan. It could walk after it had been wound up.

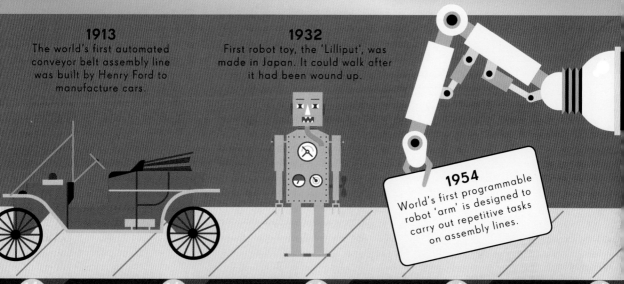

1954
World's first programmable robot 'arm' is designed to carry out repetitive tasks on assembly lines.

2000
ASIMO, a humanoid robot that can run, jump and play football, was created by Honda.

2005
Researchers at Cornell University, USA, built the first self-replicating robot – it can rebuild itself if it gets broken into pieces.

2012
Nevada Department of Motor Vehicles (USA) issues the first ever licence for a driverless car.

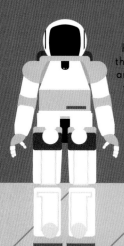

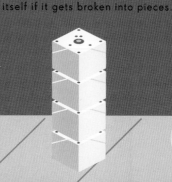

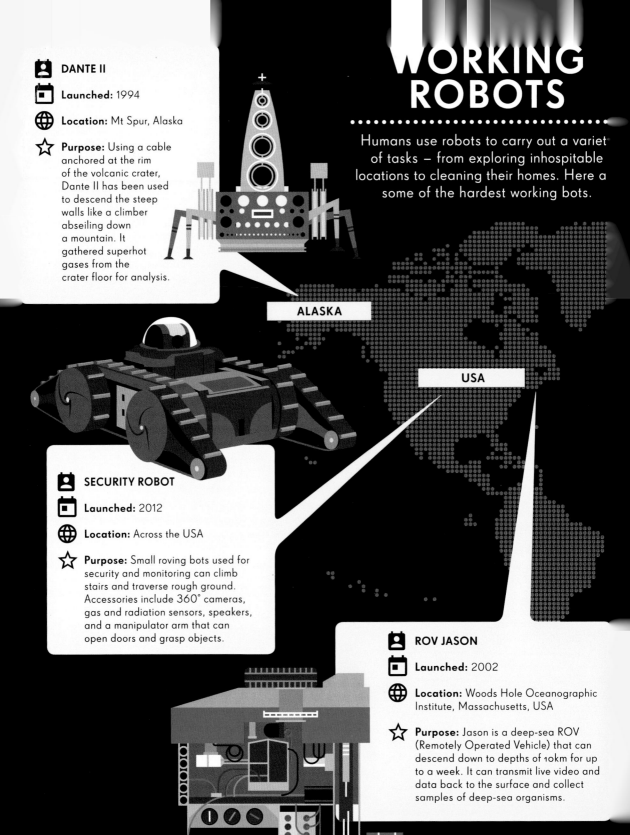

WORKING ROBOTS

Humans use robots to carry out a variety of tasks – from exploring inhospitable locations to cleaning their homes. Here a some of the hardest working bots.

DANTE II

Launched: 1994

Location: Mt Spur, Alaska

Purpose: Using a cable anchored at the rim of the volcanic crater, Dante II has been used to descend the steep walls like a climber abseiling down a mountain. It gathered superhot gases from the crater floor for analysis.

ALASKA

USA

SECURITY ROBOT

Launched: 2012

Location: Across the USA

Purpose: Small roving bots used for security and monitoring can climb stairs and traverse rough ground. Accessories include 360° cameras, gas and radiation sensors, speakers, and a manipulator arm that can open doors and grasp objects.

ROV JASON

Launched: 2002

Location: Woods Hole Oceanographic Institute, Massachusetts, USA

Purpose: Jason is a deep-sea ROV (Remotely Operated Vehicle) that can descend down to depths of 10km for up to a week. It can transmit live video and data back to the surface and collect samples of deep-sea organisms.

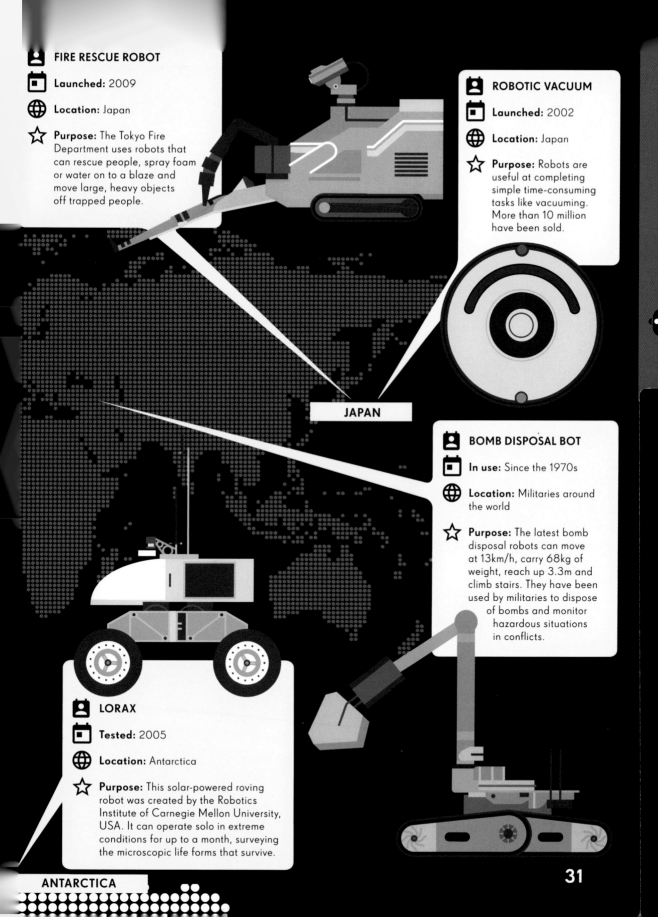

FIRE RESCUE ROBOT

Launched: 2009

Location: Japan

Purpose: The Tokyo Fire Department uses robots that can rescue people, spray foam or water on to a blaze and move large, heavy objects off trapped people.

ROBOTIC VACUUM

Launched: 2002

Location: Japan

Purpose: Robots are useful at completing simple time-consuming tasks like vacuuming. More than 10 million have been sold.

JAPAN

BOMB DISPOSAL BOT

In use: Since the 1970s

Location: Militaries around the world

Purpose: The latest bomb disposal robots can move at 13km/h, carry 68kg of weight, reach up 3.3m and climb stairs. They have been used by militaries to dispose of bombs and monitor hazardous situations in conflicts.

LORAX

Tested: 2005

Location: Antarctica

Purpose: This solar-powered roving robot was created by the Robotics Institute of Carnegie Mellon University, USA. It can operate solo in extreme conditions for up to a month, surveying the microscopic life forms that survive.

ANTARCTICA

ARTIFICIAL INTELLIGENCE

The big question within the field of robot technology asks if robots can be 'intelligent' in the way that humans are? Intelligence is being able to communicate with others using language, having knowledge and being able to solve problems. Could a thinking 'robot brain' ever be created?

BUILDING A BRAIN

The brain is made up of billions of interconnected cells called neurons, which send and receive electrical signals. Scientists are attempting to create a simulation of a working brain on a supercomputer by mapping the positions of neurons.

SEEING THINGS

Humanoid robots have cameras that function as eyes. Like humans, they have stereoscopic vision, providing sense of depth. The difficult part is programming robots to recognise what their cameras are seeing.

SAY WHAT?

Robots can be programmed to speak hundreds of languages or to talk to you continuously. However, the ability to understand speech and respond is much more complex to 'design'.

RULES OF LIFE

Sci-fi author Isaac Asimov (1920–1992) introduced the three laws of robotics in a novel in 1942. They soon became mainstream.

 A robot may not injure a human being or allow a human being to come to harm.

 A robot must obey any orders given to it by human beings, except where such orders would conflict with the First Law.

 A robot must protect its own existence as long as such protection does not conflict with the First or Second Law.

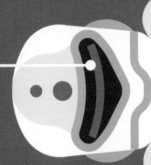

POWER UP

Humans can keep moving all day... after a big breakfast! Robots consume electricity and need to recharge their batteries every few hours. Some robots will find a charging port when they are low on power.

BALANCING ACT

Some of the most advanced humanoids can walk, run and jump. There is even a robot football competition! Balance is difficult to achieve perfectly.

THE TURING TEST

Pioneering computer scientist Alan Turing (1912–1954) created a test for measuring robot intelligence in 1950. The test assumed that a human would be able to tell apart another human from a robot using the replies of questions asked to both.

Good afternoon

THAT'S HANDY

Replicating the human hand is extremely difficult, since it can both pick a flower and punch through a plank of wood.

HELLO ASIMO

In 2000, Honda's ASIMO was the first robot to show that humanoids could live with and help humans. In the future, robots like ASIMO will be able to carry out rescues and complete practical tasks for less-abled people.

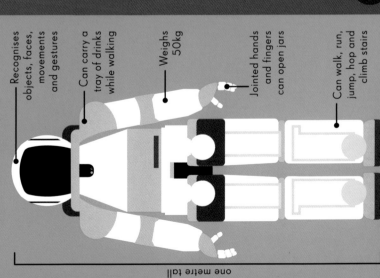

Recognises objects, faces, movements and gestures

Can carry a tray of drinks while walking

Weighs 50kg

Jointed hands and fingers can open jars

Can walk, run, jump, hop and climb stairs

one metre tall

ROBOTS IN SPACE

Robots have been used to explore distant planets and moons. Some fly past the target, some land on the target and others travel around on the extraterrestrial surface. These incredible robots are true space explorers.

PLANETARY PROBES

Since the 1960s dozens of robot probes have been sent out on missions into the Solar System and beyond to examine planets, moons, asteroids and comets. More than 20 are still operational and only a few are rovers that can travel around on the surface.

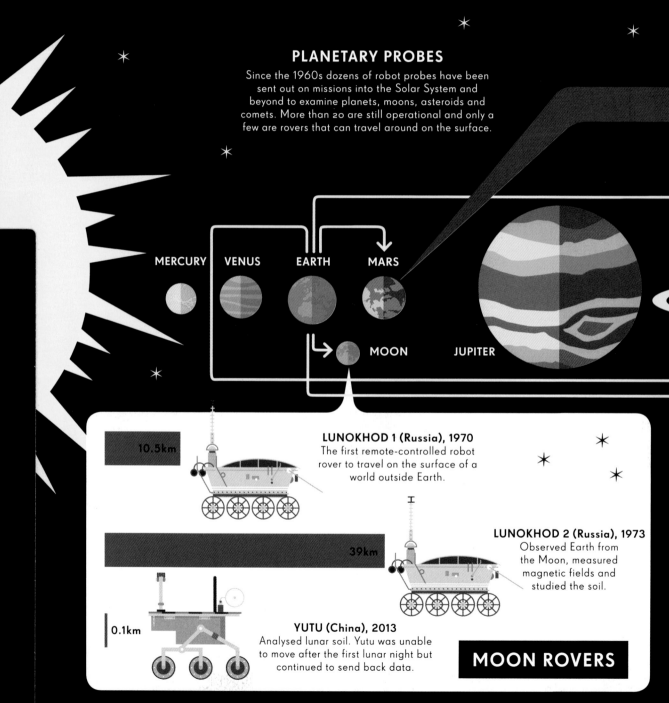

MERCURY   VENUS   EARTH   MARS

MOON   JUPITER

LUNOKHOD 1 (Russia), 1970
The first remote-controlled robot rover to travel on the surface of a world outside Earth.

10.5km

39km

0.1km

LUNOKHOD 2 (Russia), 1973
Observed Earth from the Moon, measured magnetic fields and studied the soil.

YUTU (China), 2013
Analysed lunar soil. Yutu was unable to move after the first lunar night but continued to send back data.

MOON ROVERS

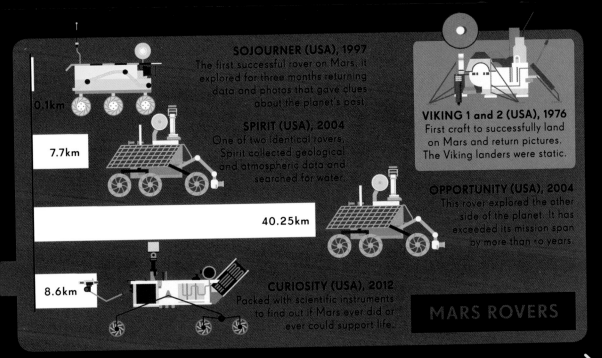

SOJOURNER (USA), 1997
The first successful rover on Mars, it explored for three months returning data and photos that gave clues about the planet's past.

0.1km

SPIRIT (USA), 2004
One of two identical rovers, Spirit collected geological and atmospheric data and searched for water.

7.7km

VIKING 1 and 2 (USA), 1976
First craft to successfully land on Mars and return pictures. The Viking landers were static.

OPPORTUNITY (USA), 2004
This rover explored the other side of the planet. It has exceeded its mission span by more than 10 years.

40.25km

8.6km

CURIOSITY (USA), 2012
Packed with scientific instruments to find out if Mars ever did or ever could support life.

MARS ROVERS

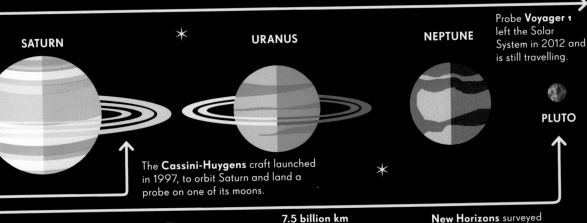

SATURN

URANUS

NEPTUNE

Probe **Voyager 1** left the Solar System in 2012 and is still travelling.

PLUTO

The **Cassini-Huygens** craft launched in 1997, to orbit Saturn and land a probe on one of its moons.

7.5 billion km

New Horizons surveyed dwarf planet Pluto in 2015.

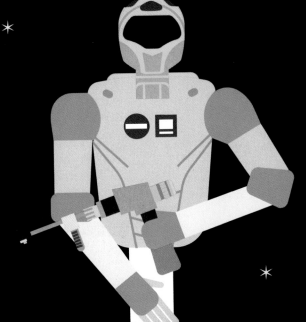

ROBONAUT!
Since 2011, scientists aboard the International Space Station (ISS) have been experimenting with a humanoid robot called Robonaut. It has robotic arms and jointed hands, so it can be programmed to perform maintenance missions in space, such as using tools to complete repairs on the outside of the ISS.

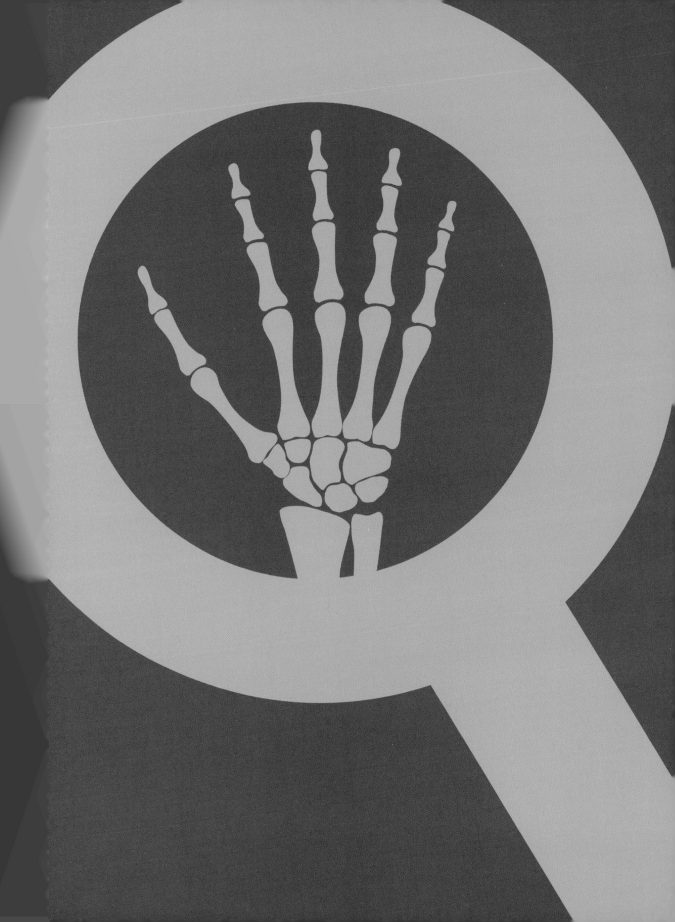

MEDICAL MARVELS

Historical records tell us that people have practised medicine for more than 10,000 years, with evidence from ancient Egypt, China and India. Treatments from these times were very different from those practised today. Up until just a few hundred years ago, knowledge of the basic workings of the human body was still relatively limited and blood-sucking leeches were administered for almost any ailment.

During the 18th and 19th centuries, a group of pioneers revolutionised medicinal science. Edward Jenner developed the first vaccine for smallpox in 1796, and in 1928 Alexander Fleming discovered penicillin – the first antibiotic. Today, you may be given a vaccine to prevent disease, or an antibiotic to fight infection.

Medical treatments of the 21st century rely on high-tech machines. MRI scanners can see what's going on inside your body, dialysis machines can clean your blood and a robot may carry out your operation, instead of a surgeon.

In the medical world scientists and doctors are saving more people than ever before. Turn the page to see how we got here.

TEN KEY DEVELOPMENTS

Advances in medicine typically take a long time. However, in recent years there have been many big strides forwards in research and treatments. Here are some of the key developments in the field of medicine.

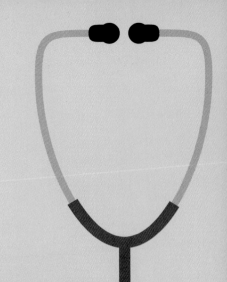

PACEMAKER (1932)

Dr Albert S. Hyman invented the first artificial pacemaker – a device that delivers electrical pulses to the heart to restart it and regulate its beat. The machine was 25cm long and powered by a hand-cranked motor.

STETHOSCOPE (1816)

Invented by French doctor René Laënnec to hear body sounds more clearly, the first model was a wooden tube that resembled an ear trumpet. Modern stethoscopes are made up of a rubber tube, two earpieces and a chestpiece. By 1850 the stethoscope had become an essential tool for every doctor.

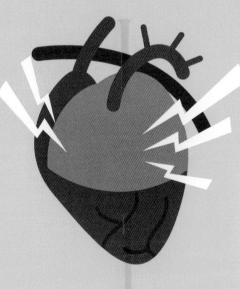

HEART TRANSPLANT (1967)

The first successful human heart transplant was a revolutionary operation at the time. Today, more than 3,500 heart transplants are performed every year.

DIALYSIS (1943)

The first dialysis machine was developed by Dutch doctor Willem Kolff during WWII to treat people with kidney disease. Blood is pumped through the machine, which – like a human kidney – filters the blood to remove toxins.

ARTIFICIAL LIVER (2006)

An artificial liver was grown using stem cells from an umbilical cord in a laboratory in England – the first was only the size of a small coin. The technique is paving the way to grow full-size organs in the future.

38

CT SCANNER (1971)

The first CT scanner was built in 1971. It combines X-ray images taken from different angles to create 3D cross-sections of a patient's body. The first CT scan image revealed a detailed picture of a living human brain.

ANAESTHESIA (1842)

The first minor operations were performed using the chemical diethyl ether as an anaesthetic. Before anaesthetic, operations were much more painful!

FOETAL ULTRASOUND (1958)

An ultrasound uses high-frequency sound waves to create an image of the patient's insides. They are most commonly used to monitor babies inside their mothers' wombs. The picture is displayed on a TV screen in black and white, colour or even 3D.

HUMAN GENOME (2003)

The mapping of the human genome – our genetic DNA blueprint – was completed after 13 years. It is helping doctors to better understand how diseases affect the body and to develop new treatments.

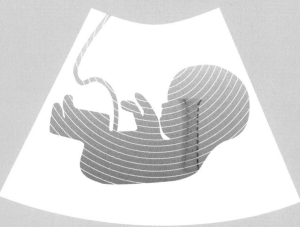

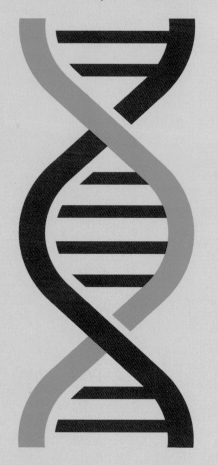

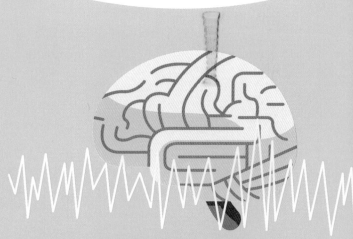

BRAIN WAVES (1875)

British scientist Richard Caton discovered the activity of electrical impulses in the brain using an electrical meter called a galvanometer. This would later lead to the development of the EEG in 1929 – a method of recording the activity in the brain using sensors attached to the head.

THE MODERN HOSPITAL

Hospitals are full of machines, monitors, robots and essential equipment, which help to diagnose diseases and keep people alive. Even the modern hospital bed is a complex piece of engineering.

LIFE SUPPORT

When a patient is unable to breathe on their own, a ventilator can carry out this function to keep them alive.

1 The ventilator pumps out clean air.

2 The air is warmed and moistened in a humidifier.

3 The ventilator uses pressure to push the air through a tube, inserted down the patient's throat, into the lungs to inflate them.

4 Exhaled breath is gently sucked away.

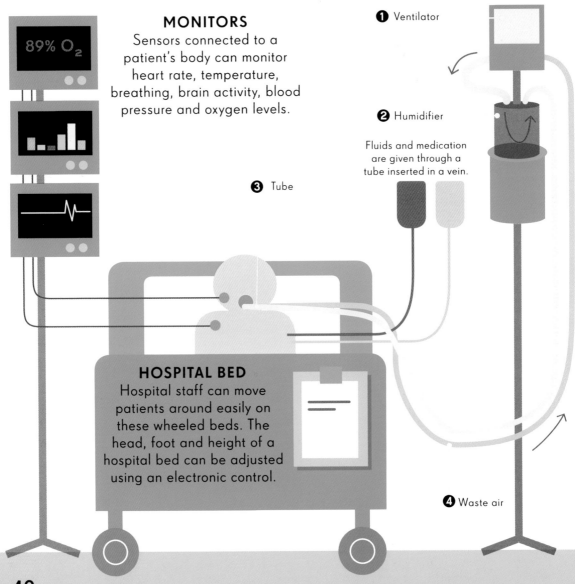

MONITORS

Sensors connected to a patient's body can monitor heart rate, temperature, breathing, brain activity, blood pressure and oxygen levels.

89% O₂

1 Ventilator

2 Humidifier

Fluids and medication are given through a tube inserted in a vein.

3 Tube

HOSPITAL BED

Hospital staff can move patients around easily on these wheeled beds. The head, foot and height of a hospital bed can be adjusted using an electronic control.

4 Waste air

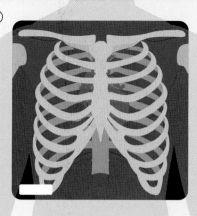

③ X-ray image

X-RAY

X-rays, a type of high-energy ray, were discovered in 1895. They are used to 'see' inside the human body.

① The patient is positioned beneath the X-ray machine. The operator stands back behind a lead screen for protection from the radioactive rays.

② An beam of X-rays is fired at the body part, on to a sensitive film below.

③ The X-rays that reach the sensitive film are developed like a photograph to create the image. Bone, fat, muscle and tissue absorb X-rays in different amounts, seen as different shades.

CT SCAN

A CT scan uses multiple X-ray 'slices' to create a 3D view inside the body without having to cut it open.

① The patient lies still on a bed that moves slowly through the cylindrical scanner.

② A fan of X-ray beams are fired from an emitter on a rotating ring inside the cylinder. They are received by X-ray detectors.

③ The ring rotates lots of times to generate hundreds of images.

④ A computer combines the X-ray image 'slices' to show a 3D view at any angle through the body.

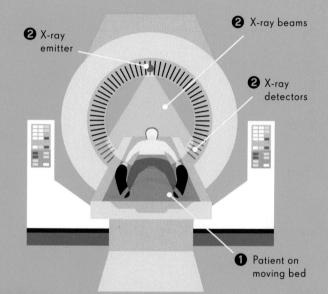

❷ X-ray emitter

❷ X-ray beams

❷ X-ray detectors

❶ Patient on moving bed

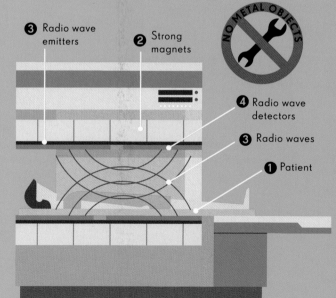

❸ Radio wave emitters

❷ Strong magnets

NO METAL OBJECTS

❹ Radio wave detectors

❸ Radio waves

❶ Patient

MRI SCAN

An MRI scanner uses strong magnets and radio waves to examine any part of the body.

① The patient lays still inside the scanner.

② Powerful magnets cause the hydrogen atoms in the patient's body to line up.

③ Pulses of radio waves are emitted, which disturbs the hydrogen atoms and knocks them out of alignment.

④ Hydrogen atoms in different tissues give different signals, which are detected and used to build an image. Even thinking can change the way your brain looks to an MRI scanner.

DOC BOTS

The cutting edge of medical science includes some incredibly complex and clever machines. Here are some of them.

DA VINCI SURGICAL SYSTEM

This $2 million robotic surgery system is equipped with specialist tools. It can be operated to perform complex operations through small incisions in the skin, which makes recovery quicker.

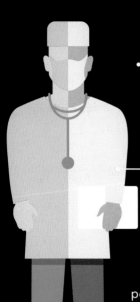

A surgeon can control a surgical robot from another room – even another continent! – using remote controls

NEUROARM

A robotic arm designed to perform brain surgery with a high level of accuracy. It was built to copy how the human hand moves, with extra precision.

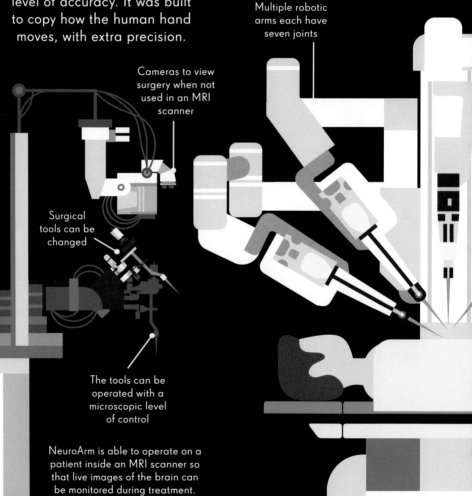

Multiple robotic arms each have seven joints

Cameras to view surgery when not used in an MRI scanner

Surgical tools can be changed

The tools can be operated with a microscopic level of control

NeuroArm is able to operate on a patient inside an MRI scanner so that live images of the brain can be monitored during treatment.

NANOBOTS

Scientists are developing tiny robots that can travel around the body in the bloodstream. Researchers hope that nanobots built entirely of DNA will help to treat critically ill leukaemia patients. These minuscule robots will be designed to seek out and destroy cancer cells.

100 nanobots could line up across this dot

CYBERKNIFE

Contrary to its name, Cyberknife is a radiation machine that treats cancer non-invasively. Its robotic arm can move around the patient delivering a high-dose beam of radiation to the exact location of the cancer.

Each robot arm has a jointed 'wrist' at the end, more flexible than a human's

3D X-ray cameras provide images during treatment

The surgeon directs the robot arms using a control panel next to the machine.

Focused radiotherapy can pinpoint tumours without harming surrounding tissue

The robot is mounted on a sturdy base

THE BIONIC HUMAN

The idea of humans with robotic arms and legs was once only imagined in science fiction. Today, vital limbs can be replaced with fully functional artificial ones.

User thinks about moving their missing limb, which triggers muscle impulses

Sensors on the skin detect the tiny electrical signals from moving muscles and change them into arm and hand movements

DEKA ARM
A sophisticated arm that can move realistically at the shoulder, elbow, wrist and fingers. It allows users to perform delicate tasks such as picking up an egg.

CYBORG BEAST
A simple fully mechanical plastic hand, controlled by the movement of the wearer's wrist and elbow. It is 3D-printed and costs around $50 to produce.

Users can choose their own colours

Cords and screws secure the movable parts of the hand together

Weighs the same as a normal arm and contains its own battery

The designs are free to download online, so the hand can be printed and assembled anywhere

44

THE MISSING LINK

New technology is allowing paralysis sufferers to control limb movement using their thoughts.

❷ Scientists implant a chip in the brain of a paralysed patient.

❸ Software decodes the brain signals read by the chip and sends them to electrodes placed on the limb, which stimulate movement

❶ Spinal injury prevents brain signals reaching the limb.

FLEX-FOOT CHEETAH

Launched in 1996, this limb is designed specifically for running and has been widely used at the Paralympics. The curved 'blade' works like a spring, storing and releasing energy with each stride.

BiOM ANKLE

This motor-driven ankle simulates the power of the lost muscle and tendons, giving the wearer a powered push off the ground when walking.

Both prosthetic limbs can be adapted for different types of amputation

The 'blade' acts as a spring to push the runner forwards with every step

Made from layers of lightweight carbon fibre, weighing 512g

Sensors constantly adjust the ankle position depending on walking speed and terrain to maintain balance

Soles have a rubber grip like a running shoe

THE PARALYMPICS

Technology has helped athletes of all abilities compete on the world stage at the Paralympics.

Prosthetic limbs: Depending on the event, different kinds of custom prosthetic limbs are worn by athletes.

Wheelchairs: Specially designed wheelchairs for high-speed races to basketball provide the manoeuvrability needed.

Archery bow: Athletes without one or both arms can fire arrows with their feet using specially designed bows.

ON THE MOVE

How do you normally get from A to B – drive, get on a train or catch a flight? Transport is part of our everyday lives and unquestionably has transformed the way the world operates.

The internal combustion engine is a marvel of engineering. It revolutionised transport when it was invented in the 1860s and has been honed over the years to peak performance. Today, we are increasingly looking for more environmentally friendly methods of transport that don't churn out clouds of pollution. Electric cars are now a reality.

Trains can travel at hundreds of kilometres per hour, with new models breaking once unimaginable speed limits. In the sky, huge airliners carry millions of people around the world every day. In the future, they may even do so without pilots, as automatically controlled flight becomes more common.

If humans decide to travel further, to planets and moons to take up home, then brand-new technologies will be required to help live a future life in deep space. We may have to get used to a journey lasting a lifetime – or a hundred lifetimes.

Turn the page to transport yourself through vehicle technology...

ON THE ROAD

Motor vehicles have come a long way since Karl Benz designed the very first car at the end of the 19th century. Some can travel at incredible speeds, others are eco-friendly and some turn off when you pause to use less fuel.

ELECTRIC
An electric car's motor is connected to a battery that has to be recharged after every 200km. Entirely battery-powered cars emit zero pollution, but don't have the power to hit high speeds.

HYBRID
A hybrid vehicle uses fuel but also has an electric motor and a battery. The battery charges as the car drives, which can be used to power the vehicle at low speeds in urban areas.

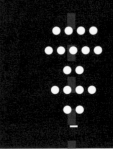

FUEL
Internal combustion is still the engine choice for most cars, which burns fuel such as petrol or diesel.

	FUEL	HYBRID	ELECTRIC
Cost to buy	●●●	●●●●	●●●
Time to fill up	●●	●●●	●●●●
Range	●●●	●●●	●●
Efficiency	●●●	●●●●	●●●●
Top speed	●●●	●●●	●●
Emissions	●●●	●●	●

> OVER 100 YEARS OF CARS

1886
Karl Benz designed the first petrol-powered automobile – a three-wheeled tricycle.

1891
The first US electric car was built by William Morrison.

1908
Ford introduced the Model T – the first low-price, mass-produced car. 15 million were sold.

1940
The Jeep four-wheel drive off-road vehicle was designed for wartime use.

THRUST SSC

The official land-speed record was set by British driver and former RAF pilot Andy Green in the Black Rock Desert, southwest USA, in October 1997. Thrust SSC was the first car ever to travel faster than the speed of sound – here's how it did it.

Length: 16.5m
Weight: 10,500kg
Engines: 2 x Rolls Royce Spey 202 (used in jet fighter planes)
Fuel: Jet fuel burning 18L/second

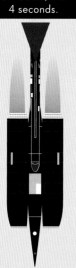

ACCELERATION
0–160km/h in 4 seconds.
1

1,000km/h after 16 seconds.
2

TOP SPEED
Thrust SSC breaks the sound barrier and hits top speed.
3

SLOWING DOWN
Begins to slow at 30km/s.
4

BOOM!

HIGH-SPEED BREAKING
Parachutes deploy, slowing the car to 500km/h quickly. However, it still takes 10km to stop.
5

TURN AND RETURN
The record is taken from an average of two runs in opposite directions, which must be completed in under an hour.
6

Average speed 1,228 kilometres per hour

1959
The iconic Austin Mini was produced – a small, economical four-seater car that gained huge popularity.

1973
First cars went on sale with a passenger airbag (driver airbags followed the next year).

1974
Electrical engineer Dr Victor Wouk built the first hybrid car.

2005
'Stanley', created at Stanford University, USA, won the DARPA Grand Challenge (driverless vehicle competition) and led to the creation of Google's self-driving car.

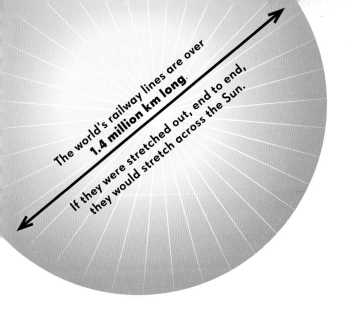

The world's railway lines are over **1.4 million km long**.

If they were stretched out, end to end, they would stretch across the Sun.

TOP TRAINS

For most countries, steam power is a thing of the past when it comes to locomotive travel. Today, high-speed Maglev (magnetic levitation) trains are a reality – and they are only set to get faster. Here are the facts about the world's train network.

MILES OF TRACKS

Laying train tracks is a feat of engineering in itself. There are one million km of track in use in the world. The five countries that have the most are:

223,000km, USA
121,000km, China
86,000km, Russia
67,000km, India
46,000km, Canada

HIGHEST RAIL STATION IN EUROPE
Jungfraujoch in Switzerland, at an altitude of 3,454m

LONGEST RAIL TUNNEL
Gotthard Base Tunnel in Switzerland is 57km long

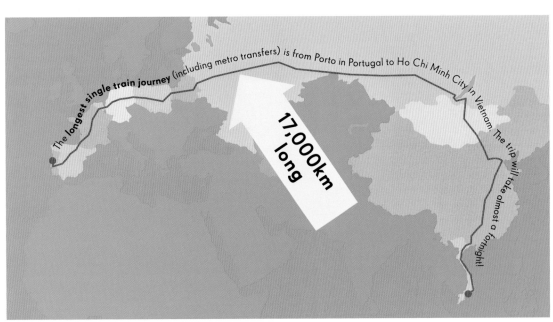

The longest single train journey (including metro transfers) is from Porto in Portugal to Ho Chi Minh City in Vietnam. The trip will take almost a fortnight!

17,000km long

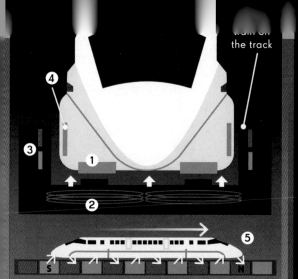

train on the track

HOW DOES A MAGLEV WORK?

S N

① Powerful magnets on the underside of the train move over coils of wire in the track. This creates a magnetic field in the coils.

② The magnetised coils in the track repel the magnets on the underside of the train with enough force to lift the train off the ground.

③ Propulsion magnets in the track walls switch their magnetic direction from north to south at the same speed as the train travelling past.

④ Magnets on either side of the train have a constant magnetic direction, allowing the switching propulsion magnets push it forwards.

⑤ Just as two poles repel each other and opposites attract, magnets on the train are pushed from behind and pulled forwards without the drag of friction, generating extremely high speeds.

FASTEST TRAINS IN THE WORLD

It's faster to take a train than to fly in some parts of the world. These trains are some of the speediest in public service.

300km/h
KTX-II
South Korea, 2010

320km/h
EUROSTAR E320
UK–France, 2015

320km/h
TGV DUPLEX
France, 1996

320km/h
E5 SHINKANSEN
Japan, 2011

330km/h
ICE3
Germany, 2000

360km/h
TALGO-350
Spain, 2007

360km/h
AGV ITALO
Italy, 2011

380km/h
CRH380A
China, 2010

420km/h
SHANGHAI MAGLEV
China, 2004

500km/h
MAGLEV
Japan, 2017

AIR ACES

Every day, more than eight million people fly across the globe. Aircraft technology has been honed to top performance in the last century, with some milestone planes along the way.

Length	6.4m
Width	12.2m
Height	2.7m
Weight	274kg
Speed	48km/h
Range	260m
Altitude	9m

12-horsepower gasoline engine

THE FIRST
Wright Flyer (1903)

American inventors Orville and Wilbur Wright created the first powered aircraft. They flew it four times on the 17 December, 1903, near Kitty Hawk, North Carolina, USA.

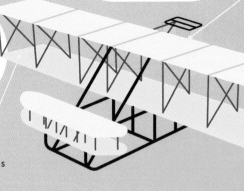

Wings covered in canvas – a design that would become standard until after World War I

The Airbus A380 is more efficient than most modern small cars when comparing fuel used and passengers miles (miles per each passenger in vehicle)

40 million
tonnes of goods are transported per year

THE BIGGEST
Airbus A380 (2005–present)

This $428-million double-decker passenger plane flies passengers all over the world. As well as being bigger, its engines are cleaner and quieter than many other aircraft.

Length	72.7m
Width	79.8m
Height	24.5m
Weight	580,000kg
Speed	945km/h
Range	15–16,000km
Altitude	13,140m

32.7m	**Length**
16.9m	**Width**
5.6m	**Height**
77,110kg	**Weight**
3,530km/h	**Speed**
5–6,000km	**Range**
25,930m	**Altitude**

THE FASTEST

Lockheed SE-71 Blackbird (1976–1998)

A stealth reconnaissance plane designed to be faster than any missile fired to destroy it. It could fly at three times the speed of sound.

Friction from the air made the titanium surface of the SE-71 as hot as 300°C after landing

The engines had to be started with controlled explosions, because the special jet fuel (for supersonic planes) was difficult to burn

3.5 trillion km

travelled by international passengers per year

17,000

passenger aircraft are in use around the world

SpaceShipTwo

is an aircraft being developed by Virgin to fly passengers into space

Length	4m
Width	4.3m
Height	1.6m
Weight	141kg
Speed	340km/h
Range	500km
Altitude	1,625m

Over 5,000 kits were sold, but only a few hundred were built

THE SMALLEST

Bede BD-5 (1960s)

This one-seater aircraft was sold in kit form for aviation fans to assemble themselves and also appeared in the James Bond film *Octopussy*.

Jim Bede designed over a dozen different aircraft

BIGGEST SHIPS

• •

Ships as big as skyscrapers exist, and they help to move millions of tonnes of goods around the world's oceans. Discover some of the vessels that have pushed the boundaries of modern engineering.

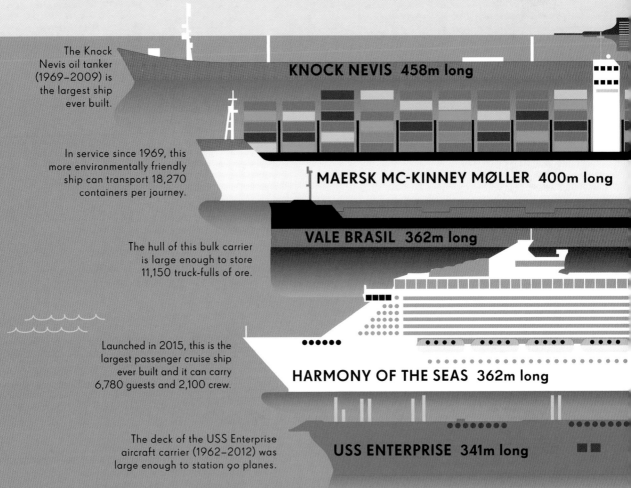

The Knock Nevis oil tanker (1969–2009) is the largest ship ever built.

KNOCK NEVIS 458m long

In service since 1969, this more environmentally friendly ship can transport 18,270 containers per journey.

MAERSK MC-KINNEY MØLLER 400m long

The hull of this bulk carrier is large enough to store 11,150 truck-fulls of ore.

VALE BRASIL 362m long

Launched in 2015, this is the largest passenger cruise ship ever built and it can carry 6,780 guests and 2,100 crew.

HARMONY OF THE SEAS 362m long

The deck of the USS Enterprise aircraft carrier (1962–2012) was large enough to station 90 planes.

USS ENTERPRISE 341m long

FASTEST BOATS

When it comes to building machines that go, humans want to travel faster than before – and it's not just about having a powerful engine. Here are some speedy boats, old and new.

SPIRIT OF AUSTRALIA
Ken Warby broke the 500km/h water speed record in 1974 in his backyard-built motorboat.

511km/h

SOVIET K-222
A record-breaker of its day in 1971, it hit a top underwater speed of any submarine.

VESTAS SAILROCKET 2
An ultra-streamlined vessel with a wing-like sail and a cockpit like that of a jet plane.

THE WORLD IS NOT ENOUGH
A luxury yacht powered by two 5,300 horsepower diesel engines.

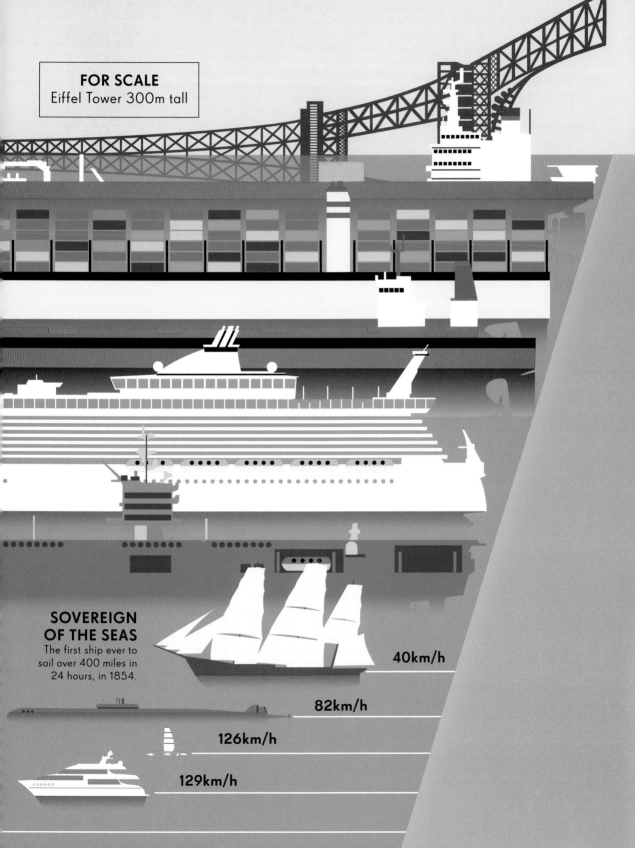

**SOVEREIGN
OF THE SEAS**
The first ship ever to
sail over 400 miles in
24 hours, in 1854.

40km/h

82km/h

126km/h

129km/h

RACE FOR SPACE

More than 500 astronauts have already made the incredible journey into space thanks to some amazing space-travelling vehicles. How has the way humans explore beyond Earth changed?

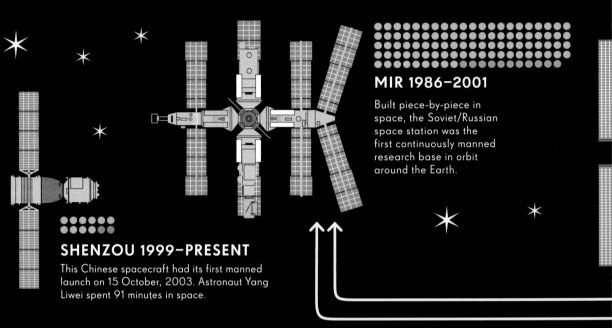

MIR 1986–2001

Built piece-by-piece in space, the Soviet/Russian space station was the first continuously manned research base in orbit around the Earth.

SHENZOU 1999–PRESENT

This Chinese spacecraft had its first manned launch on 15 October, 2003. Astronaut Yang Liwei spent 91 minutes in space.

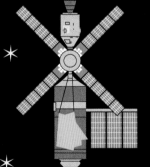

SKYLAB 1973–1979

The US's only independently built space station, Skylab was occupied for 171 days. It fell back to Earth in 1979 and broke up in the upper atmosphere.

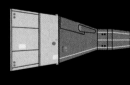

GEMINI 1965–1966

Gemini's two-man capsule transported 10 crews into space. The missions tested the astronauts' endurance and saw the first US spacewalk and docking with another craft.

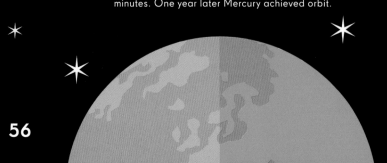

MERCURY 1959–1963

The 2m-long one-man capsule carried American Alan Shepherd into space in 1961 for 15 minutes. One year later Mercury achieved orbit.

Lunar Command Module

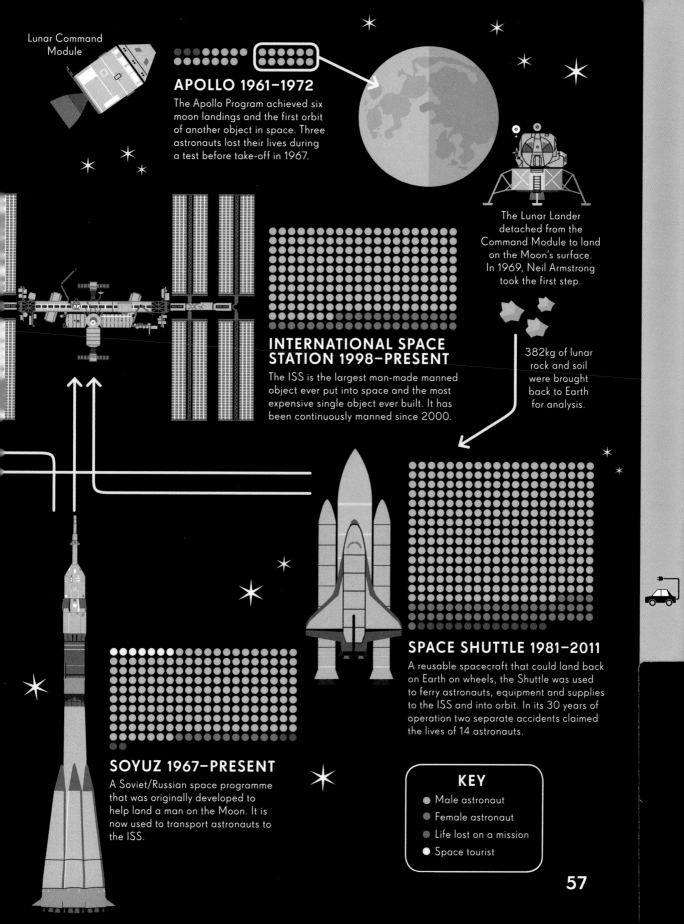

APOLLO 1961–1972

The Apollo Program achieved six moon landings and the first orbit of another object in space. Three astronauts lost their lives during a test before take-off in 1967.

The Lunar Lander detached from the Command Module to land on the Moon's surface. In 1969, Neil Armstrong took the first step.

382kg of lunar rock and soil were brought back to Earth for analysis.

INTERNATIONAL SPACE STATION 1998–PRESENT

The ISS is the largest man-made manned object ever put into space and the most expensive single object ever built. It has been continuously manned since 2000.

SPACE SHUTTLE 1981–2011

A reusable spacecraft that could land back on Earth on wheels, the Shuttle was used to ferry astronauts, equipment and supplies to the ISS and into orbit. In its 30 years of operation two separate accidents claimed the lives of 14 astronauts.

SOYUZ 1967–PRESENT

A Soviet/Russian space programme that was originally developed to help land a man on the Moon. It is now used to transport astronauts to the ISS.

KEY

- Male astronaut
- Female astronaut
- Life lost on a mission
- Space tourist

FUTURE TRAVEL

In 50 years, the way we travel could be very different from how we get around today. What are the possibilities of the cars, trains and planes of the future?

DEEP SPACE TRAVEL

Travelling far into space takes years. The journey to dwarf planet Pluto takes nine years, and to reach the next nearest galaxy would take 25,000 light years. How could humans ever make these epic journeys?

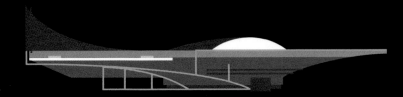

SLEEPER SHIP

We may see 'sleeper ships' full of cryopods, as seen in science-fiction films. The entire crew remain 'asleep', their bodies suspended in pods chilled to sub-zero temperatures, while the ship travels at light speed to its destination planet. There is no technology that can temporarily freeze humans – yet!

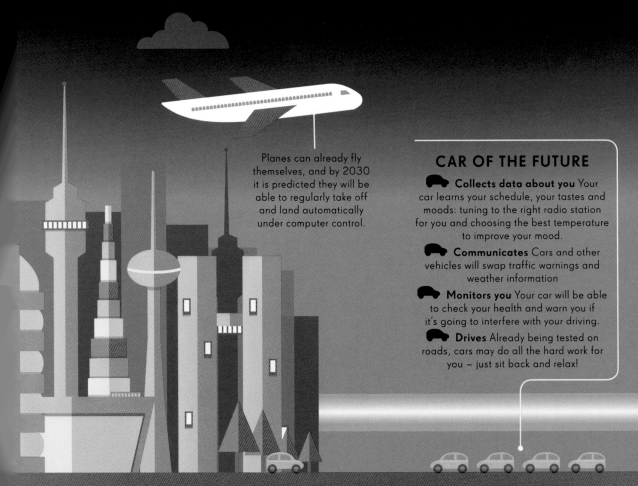

Planes can already fly themselves, and by 2030 it is predicted they will be able to regularly take off and land automatically under computer control.

CAR OF THE FUTURE

Collects data about you Your car learns your schedule, your tastes and moods: tuning to the right radio station for you and choosing the best temperature to improve your mood.

Communicates Cars and other vehicles will swap traffic warnings and weather information

Monitors you Your car will be able to check your health and warn you if it's going to interfere with your driving.

Drives Already being tested on roads, cars may do all the hard work for you – just sit back and relax!

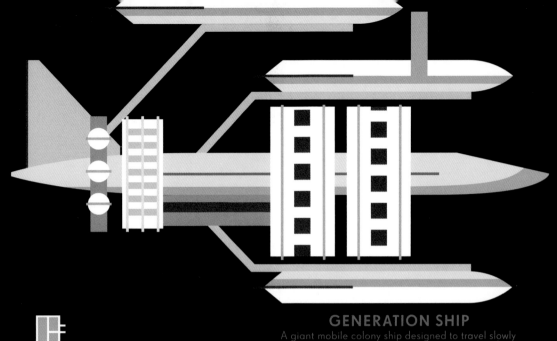

GENERATION SHIP

A giant mobile colony ship designed to travel slowly through space for hundreds or thousands of years could be the answer. As generations of people age and pass away their descendants continue the human race.

SEED SHIP

Could a ship piloted by robots containing millions of frozen human embryos populate a new planet? Robots would construct a base on the destination planet, and then unfreeze the embryos to 'grow' the population.

TRAIN OF THE FUTURE

The **Hyperloop** train concept could travel at over 1,100km/h – twice as fast as the Maglev.

Passenger 'pods' would travel in metal tubes set underground or raised on legs above.

Most of the air would be sucked out of the tubes to create a near-vacuum, cutting out air resistance.

Each pod floats on a thin cushion of air.

Air sucked in at the front of each pod is blown out of the back, propelling it along.

The technology was tested in 2016.

COMMUNICATIONS

Communication is an essential human need. From the oldest known symbols depicted on cave walls to video-calling on the latest smartphones, people have found increasingly innovative ways to pass on information over thousands of years.

The first forms of writing appeared around 6,000 years ago, made up of wedge-shaped marks made on clay tablets. Today, we can type a sentence into a mobile phone and press 'send' to communicate a message in seconds.

Messages can also be sent visually. When tall ships sailed the world's oceans in the 1800s, semaphore was used – a simple method of sending messages by waving flags that could be read from far away. Morse code, a system of short and long sound signals, was invented in the 1830s, at a time when an electrical signal could be relayed over a long distance through a single wire.

In the future, we will be even more connected with the world around us. Turn the page to find out about communication technology.

HELLO? HELLO?

Communication technology has connected long-distance friends and relatives, countries and even spacecraft. Let's go back to the beginning...

5–7 MILLION YEARS BC

Humans passed on knowledge, ancestry and stories to each other using early forms of spoken language.

38,000 YEARS BC

Humans began to record their lives in simple images on cave walls. The oldest-known cave paintings are over 40,000 years old.

3000 BC

Cuneiform, the first form of writing, was made up of wedge-shaped marks pressed into clay tablets.

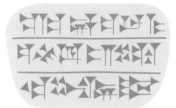

550 YEARS BC

The first large-scale postal system was set up, in Persia (now Iran). Mail (mainly from the government) could be delivered to any citizen.

150 BC

Smoke signals were used by soldiers along the Great Wall of China to alert troops to enemies. The smoke signal was relayed from tower to tower, making it visible from hundreds of kilometres away in few hours.

1440

Johannes Gutenberg developed the printing press. His version of the Bible (1455) cost three years' wages – still cheaper than a handwritten version! His invention helped the spread of learning to the masses.

1992
The first text message was sent, which said: 'Merry Christmas.' Now over 4 billion people have a mobile phone.

1960s
The US military developed a computer network system, called ARPANET, which would later form the basis of the Internet we know today.

1844
Samuel Morse sent the first telegraph message using Morse code, from Washington over 60km to Baltimore (USA). He used a device to 'click' an electrical current on and off.

2000s
Video calls became popular. Not just for work meetings or talking to distant relatives, they helped people in remote places, like astronauts. Video calling has also helped hearing-impaired people to communicate.

1990s
Computers spread everywhere and became simple enough to be used by anyone thanks to the World Wide Web, search engines, email and file sharing.

1920
The first public radio broadcast aired. By the end of the 1920s 50 million people had a radio set. Communication of news and information was now instant and wireless.

The first message sent read: 'What hath God wrought?'

POCKET POWER

Most of us carry a powerful computer around with us – the smartphone in our pocket. A step on from the mobile phone, a smartphone has many of the functions of a computer, a touchscreen and the capability to run apps.

FUNCTIONS

- Voice calls and texts
- Photo and video
- Music
- Shopping
- Banking
- Gaming
- Social networking
- Reading
- Navigation

FEATURES

- Computer-like operating system
- Large touch-screen
- Hi-resolution display
- Ability to run apps
- High-resolution camera
- Long-life compact battery
- Storage
- Stylish design
- AI assistant (e.g. Siri)

Equivalent current price
£1,100

WEIGHT
500g

PROCESSOR
Vadem 16 MHz, 16-bit, x86-compatible

TOTAL SALES
50,000

THE FIRST SMARTPHONE
The IBM Simon went on sale in 1994. It had a cutting-edge green LCD touchscreen and a stylus to navigate it. The phone included a calendar, email access, and apps that could link to a fax machine.

Average current price
£340

14:50

WEIGHT
120g

PROCESSOR
1.4GHz dual-core 64-bit

TOTAL SALES
1.4 billion

THE MODERN SMARTPHONE
More than 20 years on, devices are smaller, faster, lighter and packed with the latest processors and chips – and the technology continues to change quickly.

73% of the world's population has a mobile phone.

The **most popular use** for a phone is checking the time.

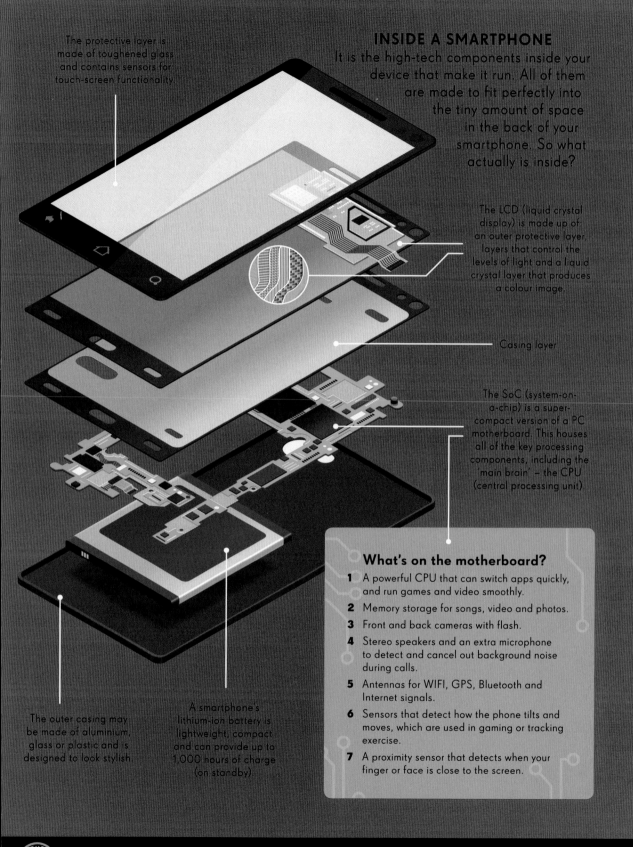

INSIDE A SMARTPHONE

It is the high-tech components inside your device that make it run. All of them are made to fit perfectly into the tiny amount of space in the back of your smartphone. So what actually is inside?

The protective layer is made of toughened glass and contains sensors for touch-screen functionality.

The LCD (liquid crystal display) is made up of: an outer protective layer, layers that control the levels of light and a liquid crystal layer that produces a colour image.

Casing layer

The SoC (system-on-a-chip) is a super-compact version of a PC motherboard. This houses all of the key processing components, including the 'main brain' – the CPU (central processing unit).

The outer casing may be made of aluminium, glass or plastic and is designed to look stylish.

A smartphone's lithium-ion battery is lightweight, compact and can provide up to 1,000 hours of charge (on standby).

What's on the motherboard?

1 A powerful CPU that can switch apps quickly, and run games and video smoothly.

2 Memory storage for songs, video and photos.

3 Front and back cameras with flash.

4 Stereo speakers and an extra microphone to detect and cancel out background noise during calls.

5 Antennas for WIFI, GPS, Bluetooth and Internet signals.

6 Sensors that detect how the phone tilts and moves, which are used in gaming or tracking exercise.

7 A proximity sensor that detects when your finger or face is close to the screen.

EXTREME COMMUNICATIONS

How does Earth communicate with far-away spacecraft? How do submarine crews deep beneath the ocean send and receive messages? How has technology helped Stephen Hawking speak again? This is extreme communications.

STEPHEN HAWKING

At 21, Professor Stephen Hawking was diagnosed with a form of Motor Neurone Disease, which made him lose the use of muscles and his voice. Since the 1980s he has used a specially designed computer to communicate.

1. A tablet computer is mounted on the arm of his wheelchair.

2. It runs a program called EZ Keys. A keyboard is displayed on the screen and a cursor scans across these letters.

3. He can stop the computer cursor by moving his cheek. This movement is detected by a sensor on his glasses.

4. EZ Keys uses an algorithm (set of mathematical calculations) that suggests the words he needs from just the first couple of characters.

5. When a sentence is finished, it is sent to his speech synthesizer, which says it out loud.

TALKING TO A SUBMARINE

Keeping in touch with submarines is tricky, not least because they are designed for stealth. Radio waves don't travel well in water, so another method of communication is needed.

VLF = Very Long Frequency signals. Long-length, slow waves that can travel up to 20m depth and send 500 words per minute.

SAFEST

Below 60m a submarine is undetectable by ships. To communicate, it can float a buoy up to just below the surface to pick up VLF waves or tow a very long antenna to receive ELF waves.

ELF = Extremely Low Frequency signals. These extra-long waves can only transmit a few characters each minute.

In 1977, **Voyager 1** and **2** were launched to explore the outer boundaries of the Solar System and beyond.

In August 2012, **Voyager 1** left our Solar System and entered deep space, travelling at over 17 km per second.

FAR-OUT VOYAGERS
Voyager 1 and 2, which are over 19 billion km away, communicate with Earth via the DSN.

DEEP SPACE NETWORK

GOLDSTONE
4 x 34m antennas
1 x 70m antenna

MADRID
1 x 26m antenna
3 x 34m antennas
1 x 70m antenna

CANBERRA
3 x 34m antennas
1 x 64m antenna
1 x 70m antenna

LONG-DISTANCE CALLING

NASA's Deep Space Network (DSN) is a global system of radio antennas, set up to track interplanetary mission spacecraft.

The DSN is made up of three sites, located in Goldstone in the USA, Madrid in Spain and Canberra, Australia.

Each location houses a 70m-wide dish antenna. The sites are spaced 120° apart around the Earth, so every direction into space is covered at all times.

IN DANGER
Submarines only surface to send and receive high-frequency radio signals, including audio and video, but in this position they are open to possible attack.

SAFER
Just below the surface a submarine is only visible to sonar – a positioning system that uses sound waves to locate objects. Subs can also pick up VLF signals at this depth.

THE FUTURE
Scientists are developing a quantum navigation system that uses a laser signal fired from a satellite to reach a submarine. The laser can track movements with 1,000 times more accuracy than GPS.

ENTERTAINMENT TODAY

Music, games, films and images are constantly being delivered to us in new and exciting ways. Whether it's the latest 3D movie, hyper-realistic video game or our favourite song, they seem ever more realistic and engaging to us.

HOW DIGITAL MUSIC FILES ARE MADE

1 In a music studio, recording equipment measures sound 96 thousand times every second. An album of raw music can be 4GB in size.

2 To convert a song into a smaller file, first the sounds that are too high and too low for humans to hear are removed.

3 Then quiet sounds that can't be heard during loud sections are also removed.

4 Finally, the sound is compressed. Now an album may take up 56Mb of memory – less than 2% of the original size.

5 Music files are ready to be distributed, on CD or online music libraries for download.

VIRTUAL REALITY GAMING

Virtual Reality (VR) puts the gamer inside a digital world. A VR headset tracks which way the user is looking, creating a 360° view of the world.

VR headset

Tracking works out which way the user is looking

3D audio helps trick the brain into believing the images are real

A treadmill allows player to walk, run, duck and jump in the gameplay

Fake tool or weapon that mimics that used in the virtual world

AUGMENTED REALITY

Augmented Reality (AR) enhances a person's view of the real world, by adding a layer of digital information or entertainment on top of it. Apps and high-tech glasses have utilised this technology.

GPS identifies relevant data based on the user's location

A tiny projector displays data on one lens of the glasses

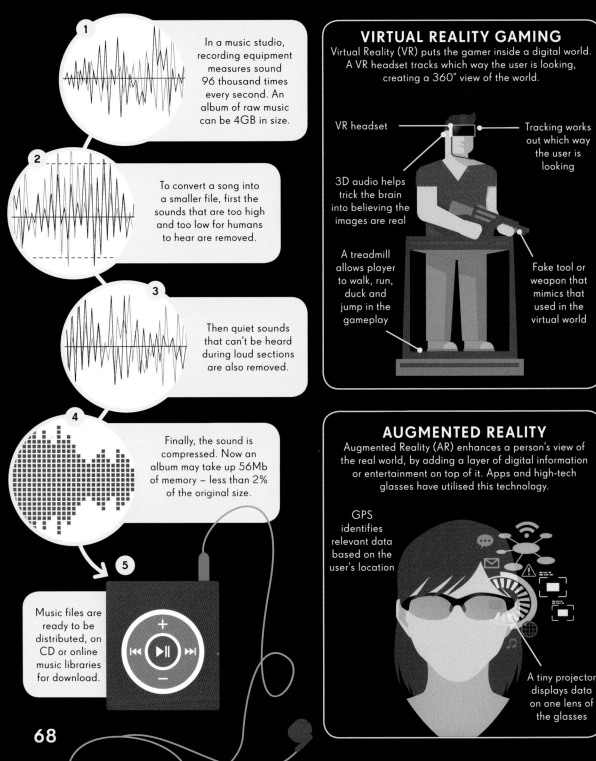

MOTION-CAPTURE ANIMATION

Motion capture (Mo-cap) is a way of digitally recording movements using sensors on the body. It is used in military, sport and medicine, but its most common use is in computer-generated animation.

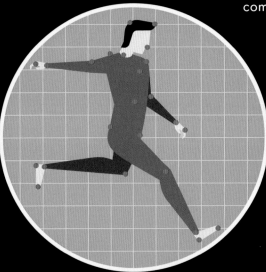

Stage 1 The actor wears a bodysuit mounted with reflective ping pong ball-sized markers on each joint. Scenes are recorded from different angles in a studio marked out with a grid.

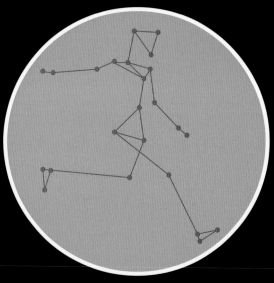

Stage 2 The recordings are combined using a computer program to create an animation of a moving 3D 'wireframe skeleton'.

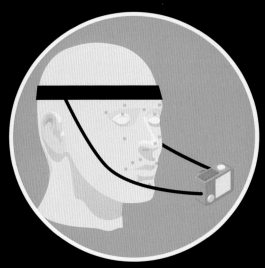

Stage 3 Cameras mounted on the actor's head record the actor's expressions as they speak and react. This is called performance capture. The actor's face is photographed from all angles to create an accurate digital model.

Stage 4 The character is built up from the different digital recordings. Performance capture imagery, costumes and even whole new animated bodies are digitally built on to the wireframe skeletons. The result – incredibly realistic computer-generated characters.

CUTTING-EDGE COMMS

The world has never been so connected – we can look around ancient Rome from the comfort of our living room, video call distant friends and check what our pet is up to while we're at work. What might the future of communication be like?

3G

4G

5G

5G IS COMING

The fifth generation of mobile network is on its way, and it's set to revolutionise communication. 5G will have the capacity to handle more than 100 billion device connections and will provide superfast connectivity.

1000 x faster than 4G

THE INTERNET OF THINGS

The Internet of Things is the ever-growing web of Internet-connected devices. In the future, even more of our world will be connected:

Supermarket tills → Warehouses
Weather satellites → Combine harvesters
Electricity meters → Power stations

THE POWER OF THE MIND

Could it ever be possible to send a thought directly into someone else's brain? Scientists are working on a technology that could allow just that. It is based on implanting a tiny silicon chip on the brain that would enable information to be downloaded.

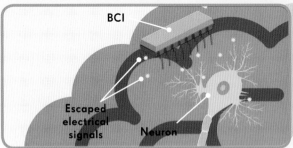

BCI

Escaped electrical signals

Neuron

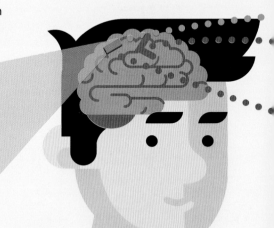

BRAIN-COMPUTER INTERFACE (BCI)

Our brains are filled with a network of neurons (nerve cells). Every time we think, move, feel, smell or remember, electrical signals zip from neuron to neuron at lightning speed. Some signals escape from the neurons, and a BCI could detect these and send them to another person.

WHEN?
2020

COST
$17 trillion (estimated)

HOW FAST?
10 GB/second
(4G 130 Mb/second)

DOWNLOAD TIME
A 2-hour film will
download in 4 seconds

HOLOGRAMS

Video calling may soon be a
thing of the past. Holographic
technology has already been
used to put late pop stars,
such as Michael Jackson, back
on the stage. You could soon
be able to have a conversation
with a picture-perfect 3D
image of the person you're
talking to, projected in the air
in front of you.

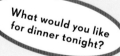

DISTANT FUTURE...

One day people
may be able to
communicate with
each other by
thought alone.

NEAR FUTURE...

Scientists are working on technology that
could use those escaped electrical signals
to control a device such as a computer.
This would be a huge breakthrough for
people with movement disabilities.

TOMORROW'S WORLD

The 21st century has seen a flurry of new electronic devices – smaller, faster and ever more portable.

What will come next? Our clothes may become the next addition to the Internet of Things, connecting with apps, devices and us. Wearable technology already exists and it is becoming more and more sophisticated. Maybe it will become part of us – a chip embedded in your arm that stores your personal data. You would never have to carry a passport again!

Your home will communicate with you – you will be able to control the heating, the oven and other appliances from any location in the world. You may even be able to print your food, instead of going to the supermarket.

Life in the future will be very different to the way we live now – but some of this unusual technology is already available. Turn the page to find out what the future could hold.

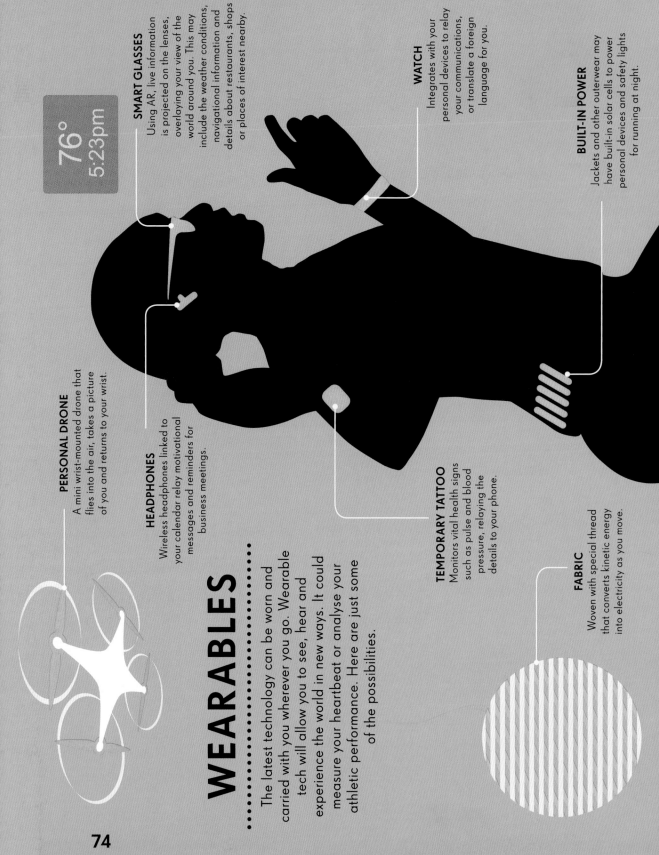

76°
5:23pm

WEARABLES

The latest technology can be worn and carried with you wherever you go. Wearable tech will allow you to see, hear and experience the world in new ways. It could measure your heartbeat or analyse your athletic performance. Here are just some of the possibilities.

PERSONAL DRONE
A mini wrist-mounted drone that flies into the air, takes a picture of you and returns to your wrist.

HEADPHONES
Wireless headphones linked to your calendar relay motivational messages and reminders for business meetings.

SMART GLASSES
Using AR, live information is projected on the lenses, overlaying your view of the world around you. This may include the weather conditions, navigational information and details about restaurants, shops or places of interest nearby.

WATCH
Integrates with your personal devices to relay your communications, or translate a foreign language for you.

BUILT-IN POWER
Jackets and other outerwear may have built-in solar cells to power personal devices and safety lights for running at night.

TEMPORARY TATTOO
Monitors vital health signs such as pulse and blood pressure, relaying the details to your phone.

FABRIC
Woven with special thread that converts kinetic energy into electricity as you move.

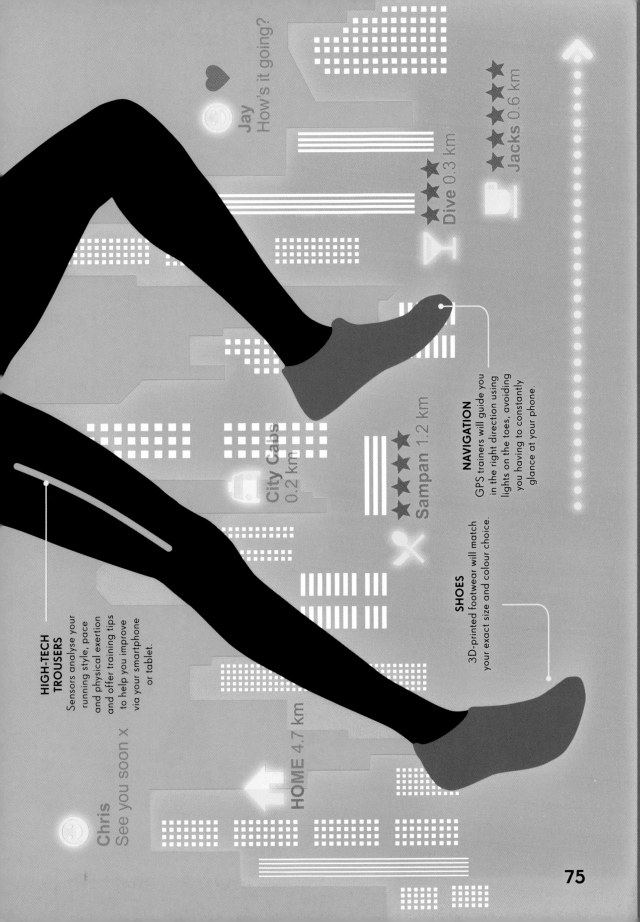

Jay
How's it going?

Dive 0.3 km

Jacks 0.6 km

NAVIGATION
GPS trainers will guide you in the right direction using lights on the toes, avoiding you having to constantly glance at your phone.

Sampan 1.2 km

City Cabs
0.2 km

SHOES
3D-printed footwear will match your exact size and colour choice.

HIGH-TECH TROUSERS
Sensors analyse your running style, pace and physical exertion and offer training tips to help you improve via your smartphone or tablet.

Chris
See you soon x

HOME 4.7 km

3D PRINTING

From everyday items to food and even body parts, 3D printing machines are making them. It's a technology that has many useful applications. Buildings could be 3D printed on an industrial scale in the future and food printers could help tackle famine in poor countries.

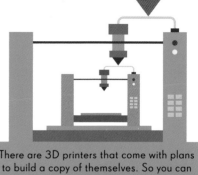

There are 3D printers that come with plans to build a copy of themselves. So you can print as many printers as you need!

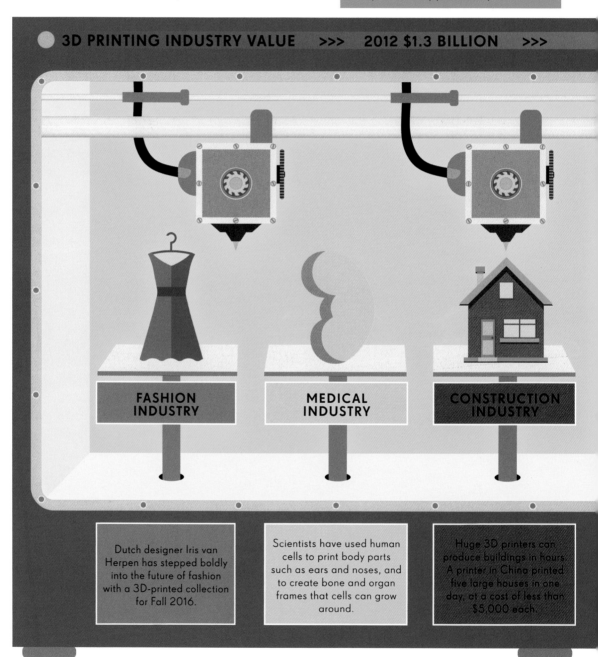

3D PRINTING INDUSTRY VALUE   >>>   2012 $1.3 BILLION   >>>

FASHION INDUSTRY

MEDICAL INDUSTRY

CONSTRUCTION INDUSTRY

Dutch designer Iris van Herpen has stepped boldly into the future of fashion with a 3D-printed collection for Fall 2016.

Scientists have used human cells to print body parts such as ears and noses, and to create bone and organ frames that cells can grow around.

Huge 3D printers can produce buildings in hours. A printer in China printed five large houses in one day, at a cost of less than $5,000 each.

HOW 3D PRINTING WORKS

1. An object is scanned...

...or a new object is designed on a computer.

2. Plastics, metals, ceramics, paper and food can be used as printing materials.

3. The printer nozzle deposits the material in layers.

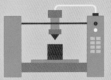

4. The object is built up layer by layer until complete.

2016 $3.1 BILLION   >>>   2020 $5.2 BILLION

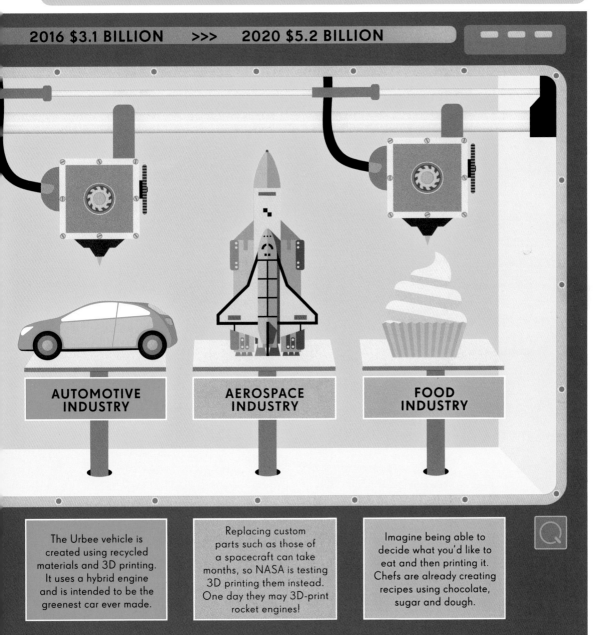

AUTOMOTIVE INDUSTRY

AEROSPACE INDUSTRY

FOOD INDUSTRY

The Urbee vehicle is created using recycled materials and 3D printing. It uses a hybrid engine and is intended to be the greenest car ever made.

Replacing custom parts such as those of a spacecraft can take months, so NASA is testing 3D printing them instead. One day they may 3D-print rocket engines!

Imagine being able to decide what you'd like to eat and then printing it. Chefs are already creating recipes using chocolate, sugar and dough.

IN THE BIN?

As the world advances, old technology is discarded. You probably remember things that will never be popular again. What is going to go next?

ON THE WAY OUT

1. CDs & DVDs
2. Newspapers
3. Incandescent light bulbs
4. Phone books
5. Public phone boxes
6. Fax machines
7. Travel agents
8. Paper maps

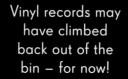

ALREADY GONE

1. Typewriters
2. Encyclopaedias
3. Negative film
4. VCRs & video tapes
5. Floppy disks
6. Old monitors & TVs
7. Dial telephones
8. Cassette tapes

Vinyl records may have climbed back out of the bin – for now!

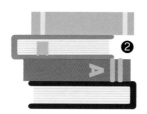

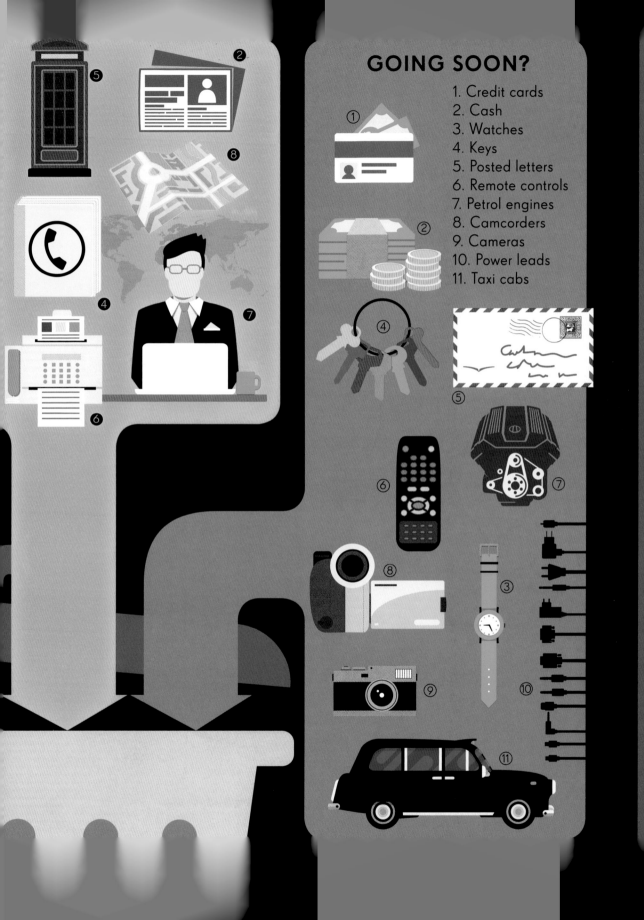

GOING SOON?

1. Credit cards
2. Cash
3. Watches
4. Keys
5. Posted letters
6. Remote controls
7. Petrol engines
8. Camcorders
9. Cameras
10. Power leads
11. Taxi cabs

B P P

BIG PICTURE PRESS

First published in the UK in 2017
by Big Picture Press, part of the
Bonnier Publishing Group, The Plaza,
535 King's Road, London, SW10 0SZ

www.bigpicturepress.net
www.bonnierpublishing.com

10 9 8 7 6 5 4 3 2 1

ISBN 978-1-78370-448-4

This book was typeset in Super Grotesk
The illustrations were created digitally

Design and additional graphics: Perfect Bound Ltd
Consultant: Steve Parker
Managing Editor: Carly Blake
Additional illustrations used under license from
Shutterstock.com

Printed in China

Studio Muti is a creative studio founded in 2011, based in the city of Cape Town, South Africa. They are a dedicated team of illustrators and designers who are passionate about producing original and inspiring artwork, from lettering to icons, digital painting to animation. Muti's large client list includes Nike, Google and Lonely Planet.

Simon Rogers edited and created guardian.co.uk/data, probably the world's most popular data journalism website and online data resource. Publishing hundreds of raw data sets, it encourages its users to visualise and analyse them. He has previously worked at Twitter in San Francisco as the organisation's first Data Editor.